My North End Family Stories

La gioia e il dolore

By

Margaret Fucillo

Copyright © 2023, Margaret Fucillo

ALL RIGHTS RESERVED.
No part of this publication may be reproduced, stored in a retrieval system or transmitted in any form or by any means whatsoever, whether electronic, mechanical, magnetic recording, or photocopying, without the prior written approval of the Copyright holder or Publisher, excepting brief quotations for inclusion in book reviews.

Published by:

Janaway Publishing, Inc.
732 Kelsey Ct.
Santa Maria, California 93454
(805) 925-1952
www.janawaygenealogy.com

2023

Front Cover: Michelina Angelina

ISBN: 978-1-59641-472-3

Made in the United States of America

TABLE OF CONTENTS

Chapter 1: Life in the North End 1

Chapter 2: A Look Around the North End 11

Chapter 3: Grandma Nonna 25

Chapter 4: Michelina Angelina: My Mama 39

Chapter 5: My Daddy Joe 47

Chapter 6: The Relatives 55

Chapter 7: Auntie Anna, Uncle Tony,
  Cousins Ron and Tony 67

Chapter 8: "You Don't Like the Food?" 77

Chapter 9: Reflections 81

Chapter 10: Research, Documents 89

Epilogue 98

About the Author 99

For Further Reading 100

Acknowledgements

Thank you to my North End Neighborhood, Saint Anthony's and Saint Leonard's Churches, Sacred Heart Church and Saint Stephen's Church. But foremost to the immigrants who braved the arduous and treacherous journey, leaving behind all they had known and their precious families, to seek a better life.

"Give me your tired, your poor,
Your huddled masses yearning to breathe free,
The wretched refuse of your teeming shore.
Send these, the homeless, tempest-tost to me,
I lift my lamp beside the golden door!"

"The New Colossus" by Emma Lazarus 1883
Engraved at the base of the Statue of Liberty

Finally, thank you to Anthony Riccio, who read my first story and told me these stories need to be told as we are "the last generation who actually lived with our parents and/or grandparents and learned their ways".

But now I have no one to ask…

To my daughter Gabriella, my Parents, Michelina and Joseph, my Grandma Nonna, Vincenza, my Auntie Jennie and my Uncle Tony.

Te voglio bene assaje, a tutti.

Prologue

My family's story in the North End begins with the arrival of my Grandfather Teodoro Fuccillo in 1881. My father's family was from the small town of Chiusano di San Domenico in the province of Avellino. My maternal grandmother's family the Iuiluccis, arrived from the larger town of Airola, in the province of Benevento in 1901. My grandmother, her two sisters and their mother and father all arrived together.

Fortunately, my mother had various documents and a very good memory to complement those documents. My grandmother lived in our building, so I also had stories from her and knew my two Great Aunts as well. So, my mother's side of the family is rich in detail and memories. However, my father's parents died before I was born.

My grandfather, Teodoro Fucillo, bought a brand new tenement in 1893. How quickly this "street laborer" achieved the American dream! He spoke no English, could not read or write in either English or Italian. My grandmother, Giusippina stayed home with her four boys and only spoke Italian, she was not able to read and write in any language. Neither of my father's parents became Naturalized citizens. None of the boys, Ralph, John, Louis or my father Joseph was educated in the United States. But they all learned to speak, read and write English in addition to reading and writing in Italian. My father was the last child born late in life to my grandparents and the only child to be born in the United States.

My mother would marry my father in 1935. However, these two families' immigration stories could not be more different.

I welcome you to enjoy, laugh and perhaps cry as you read their stories.

My North End Family Stories: La gioia e il dolore.

Chapter 1

Life in the North End

When I was growing up there was a special religious indulgence you could earn on Holy Thursday, during Holy Week. You had to walk to seven churches. Now in the North End we had it made! I mean even now if you stand on the corner of Prince and Hanover Streets you can see three churches: Sacred Heart, Saint Stephen's and Saint Leonard's. But when I was young there were also Saint Anthony's downstairs from Saint Leonard's (that counted as two churches because they had different names) and Saint Mary's on Endicott Street. We walked a bit to Saint Joseph's in the West End and we had six. Then we walked downtown and ended at Saint Anthony's Shrine! We got a ticket straight to heaven, every year!

This is all to show how small the North End really is. Geographically the North End is very compact. But at the height of Immigration 44,000+ people lived there. How did they all fit in only 0.36 square miles? The answer is: very closely.

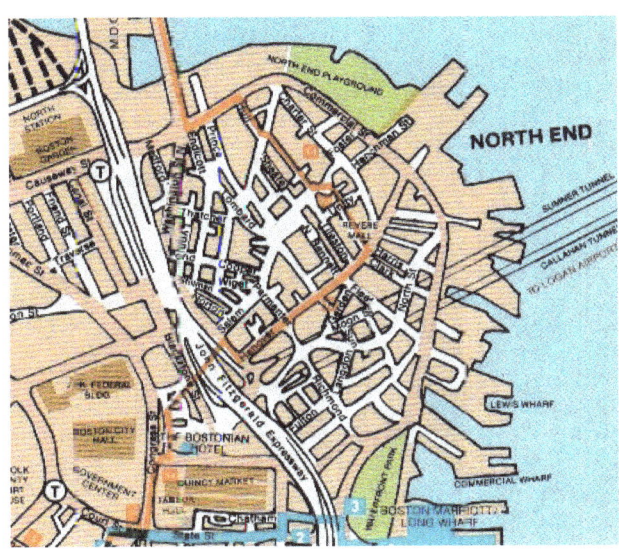

Courtesy of Vito Aluia

Prince Street

Cooper Street: The name of Jewish Owner remains on the building. "Segel"

Living Conditions, Health, and Domestic Abuse

In the 1950's, my tenement building had 8 people living in it and a bakery. But in the 1920's a Boston Globe article stated that there was a fire in the building and 30 people were evacuated. Think of an average of 10 people on each floor and one toilet in the hallway. Heat was from a coal stove and that was IF you could afford the coal. There was no hot water. These close conditions, exacerbated by little or no ventilation, led to poor hygiene, caused health issues especially respiratory and gastrointestinal diseases.

THIRTY FLEE A NORTH END FIRE

Firemen Carry Several From 19 Fleet St

Thirty persons, about one-half of whom were children, were forced to flee for safety this morning, when a brisk fire broke out on the second floor of the four-story dwelling at 19 Fleet st, North End. Before it was brought under control, damage of more than $2500 had resulted.

Flames and smoke were discovered pouring out from the rear of the second floor near the staircase, by residents on the upper floor. In a moment, the house was filled with smoke and was a bedlam of hurrying, frightened persons.

Fifteen or 20 on the upper two floors immediately made for the fire escapes and ran over to other buildings and roofs, while several were carried to the street by the firemen. People living on the first and second floors were able to get out much easier, but some were forced to resort to the escapes, owing to the dense smoke.

The firemen were forced to break down doors and walls to get at the fire. They had a busy time for a while when they were told that John di Angelis, who lives on the second floor, was still in the building. A thorough search was made and John could not be found in the upper apartment. He was later discovered, safe, in the basement.

The building, which is owned by Glotio Pucello, houses six families. On the lower floor is a shop owned by Carpinella, the florist, and considerable damage was suffered there by smoke and water.

Fortunately, there were public baths and health centers started by benevolent societies. But these were not sufficient to contain the Flu Epidemic of 1918-1920 or prevent other diseases from spreading. One of the worse tragedies was the rate of infant mortality. In my father's family three children died and in my mother's family, one child died. And I am sure more would have died had my grandfather lived.

Another issue that was never acknowledged and is only just being addressed today, is domestic abuse. I know this happened in three of my aunts' families and in my own. During this era this was a shameful subject that was not allowed to be mentioned. Somehow it was always the woman's fault or everyone knew that the husband was an alcoholic and "no good" to begin with. Sometimes the North End would Self Police and these abusers would be punished. But more often than not, wives and children suffered and shielded themselves in silence. Children would come to school emotionally broken and physically battered and bruised. Wives covered their faces when outside to shop and would wear shawls even in the hottest days of summer to cover their arms, or they did not go out at all. Abuse was internalized by women and caused more problems for the victims later in life, which would manifest itself in many ways. Today many would be diagnosed with Post Traumatic Stress Disorder.

Crime: My Family and My Best Friend

Although the North End was probably the safest place to live in Boston, it did have its problems. Neighborhood people did Self Police in the North End. However there were groups that sponsored illegal betting and "helped" people financially in need. Loans were given out at very high interest rates. They also provided "protection" for store owners so that their stores would not be robbed or vandalized. As time went on these associations were organized and evolved into more elaborate enterprises.

Most residents of the North End knew all about the bribery and shake downs. Not many were untouched. To say that this organization was good for the neighborhood, as some would attest, it is unfortunately outweighed by the bad. I don't know the extent of the "bad" as far as my family is concerned, but my uncle was a member. When his aunt passed away, we had all we could do to keep the newspapers and television away from his mother, my Zia Michelina. This news would be too much for her to bear while she was mourning the death of her sister. The news broke the same week as the wake and funeral.

My mother grew up with many members, including the heads of the major crime family. I had two very close friends and we all went to school together. We never knew how our lives were intertwined and how we would know such sorrow in future years. Lorraine was related to me through my paternal grandmother's family the Reppuccis and Thais was the daughter of the head of the major crime family in Boston. When her father was on the front page of the papers in 1963, I know how it affected my dear friend and how much she loved her father and her grandmother. She and I were together almost all our lives: school, summers at the beach, swim meets, basketball team, Saturdays, and summer camp. In September of 1969, I was in my last year of college and Thais was in her last year of Nursing School. We were only able to talk on the phone the night of her 21st birthday instead of going out to celebrate. A few days later, I received a phone call late at night. My best friend had suddenly died of an undiagnosed heart problem a few days after celebrating her 21st birthday. Lorraine and I walked into Langone's Funeral Parlor, numb with grief and in our hands we carried a dozen red roses to say our final goodbye. I honestly don't know how we were able to do that. The next day my mother came with me and we talked in Italian to Thais's Grandmother, but she just kept crying. Her father never talked to anyone. He just stood stoically next to his daughter away from the seated family members. This was one of the saddest moments in my life, one I don't think I ever shared publicly or will ever erase from my mind. We will meet again.

Thais, age 15

Poverty and Despair

People who immigrated to the North End were poor, mostly uneducated, and unskilled. Families lived in poverty and desperately wanted a better life for themselves, their families here and their families back home. People took in borders in their small, already overcrowded flats. Most men worked as heavy laborers on the docks, paving roads, digging the paths for trains and then laying the train tracks, (pick and shovel jobs). The labored many hours a day for very little money. The Sicilians were fishermen, recreating the same lives they had in Sicily.

This was not the vision most had of what would occur when they started their new lives in America. For some, the American Dream was never achieved. Poverty took its pleasure in alcohol, crime and ultimately homelessness, sickness, and death. The despair that people endured, fearing they would lose their job, that they would never have enough food or be able to sleep in a bed or be injured on their job, was prevalent among many. The stress caused some to turn to violence, to give up and abandon their families, to secure money through loans they could not pay back or to gamble, all of which destroyed families. The result caused mental health issues: fear of abandonment, failure, and hunger. This led to anger and depression. One afternoon, when I was about twelve, I went into a flat and saw my friend's father just sitting in the kitchen, never talking, just staring out the window. He was slowly shutting down and no one could help this man whose life was consumed with misery.

Let it Shine

If you didn't have a lot, make what you have shine. That must be inspired from the Patron Saint of Cleanliness, Saint Zita! Every day in the North End was cleaning day. The flats would shine. Dishes and pots sparkled, and freshly washed laundry hung outside the windows to dry on ropes with pulleys attached to another building. Stairs were swept, scrubbed and scoured as were the sidewalks and streets outside each tenement. I think that was ingrained in my mother as a child coming from Italy. My grandmother and her two daughters' two room, cold water flat had a kitchen with a sink and a bedroom with one bed where Grandma, Auntie Susie and my mother slept. Add to that, there were the three dogs and Kitty Boy the cat. The tiny space was spotless. Let it shine!

Nonna on the roof

Discrimination

Immigrants from the Southern Italy were considered inferior to the Northern Italians who had preceded the Southerners' journey to America. The Southern Italians, anyone south of Rome, were poor, generally tenant farmers, mostly unskilled and uneducated. And the Sicilians were even considered less worthy than the mainland Southern Italians. Sicilians were even at times considered another race.

So for the newly arrived immigrants the way to prosperity and respectability was to work as hard as you could and to have everyone in the flat working as soon as they were able. To spend time in school was not as important as working, making money and owning a home! The notion of even buying a home was a dream, out of the realm of possibility. Yet for many including my father's family, the dream came true.

Participation in politics, mostly controlled by the Irish in these neighborhoods, was not seen as a way forward. That political involvement would come in later years and my father would eventually run for an elected office, State Senator.

My parents, grandparents and great grandparents experienced rejection, humiliation, bigotry and even violence once they arrived in America. Not just my family but all immigrants. Although my family's experiences were sometimes even frightening, they endured the pain it caused in order to reach their goal of a better life. They are the Immigrants that prevailed.

My maternal great grandfather was the manager or perhaps even owned a restaurant/hotel in Benevento where the King, Victor Emmanuel, who had a summer residence nearby, frequented. My grandmother could read and write, very unusual for women during this time. Outwardly, this does not seem like the typical peasant immigrant family. Yet Sabatino Iuliucci uprooted his wife and three daughters in their early 20's to come to America in 1901. He was a "Boot Black" when he first came to Boston. He shined boots, perhaps on a corner. The goal was to get the daughters settled into good marriages. That goal failed. Two of my great aunts married less than admirable men, one worse than the other. And my grandmother married my grandfather who died of Tuberculosis three years after their marriage. It wasn't until my mother's generation that the upward movement to the dream that was to be had in America came into focus.

Name:	Sabatino Iuliucci
Residence Year:	1916
Street Address:	364 North
Residence Place:	Boston, Massachusetts, USA
Occupation:	Bootblack
Publication Title:	Boston, Massachusetts, City Directory, 1916

City of Boston Document

World War 2

Life became very difficult for Italian immigrants during World War 2. When Italy joined Germany in fighting the Allies and the Axis Powers subsequently declared war on the United States, discrimination against immigrants, that had eased somewhat was revived. Many Italians were fired from their jobs. Even Italians who were born in the United States were also subject to this new bigotry. The rise of "Patriotism" encouraged by President Roosevelt's speeches, energized this Anti-Italian sentiment.

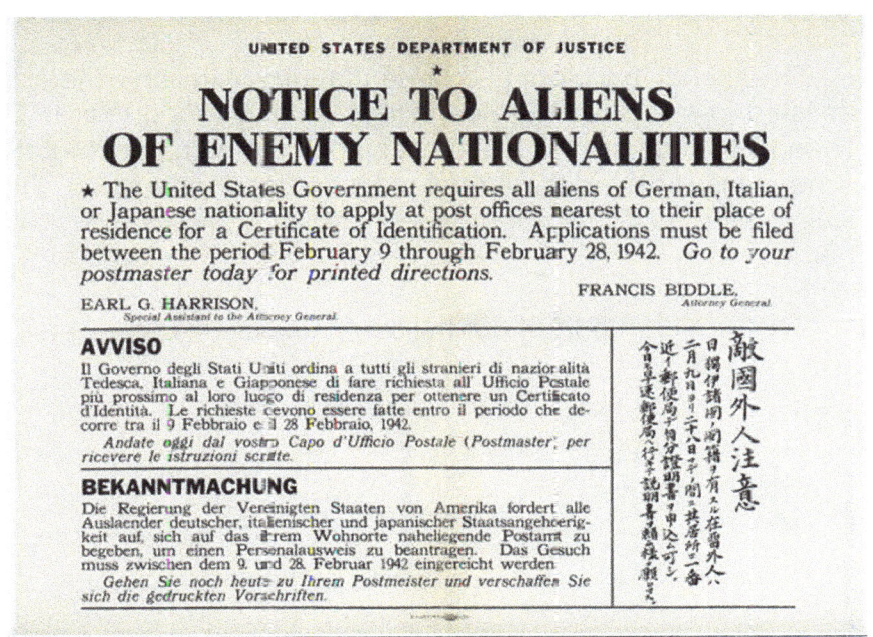

Government Sign

After the attack on Pearl Harbor, December 7, 1941. President Roosevelt signed the infamous Proclamation 2527, which stated that the approximately 600,000 Italians who were not Naturalized Citizens were "Enemy Aliens". Many Italians were put in detention camps. All Italians who had not yet applied to become naturalized citizens were encouraged very strongly to do so as soon as possible. The penalty for not complying could be deportation or being sent to internment camps. My mother helped many relatives in my father's family to apply for naturalization, Uncle Louis, Zia Michelina, and Zia Concilia, her sister in particular. My maternal grandmother also applied. I have the Naturalization records of many of my relatives. There was also a loyalty oath that had to be signed which also stated the newly naturalized citizen would renounce King Victor Emmanuel.

Due do considerable backlash and the fear of losing votes, the Proclamation was reversed, but many Italians continued to lose their jobs. Italians, whether they were citizens or not, were seen as traitors and stereotypes and prejudice from the past were rekindled.

Despite all this bigotry, a large number of Italian Americans enlisted in the United States military during World War II. Between 750,000 and 1.5 million served in the war, and 14 Italian Americans received the Medal of Honor for their service. Tragically, my Uncle Tony's brother, Uncle Angelo never came home.

This is a grim part of our Italian American History.

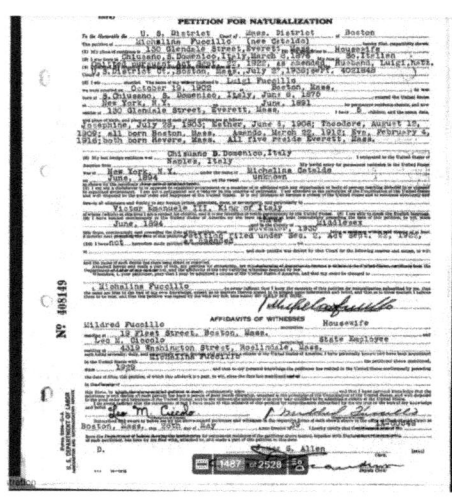
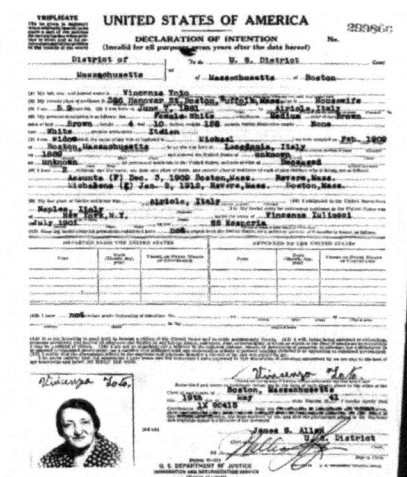

Family Documents

Chapter 2

A Look Around the North End

Town, Provinces, Region
and Then Country

My father's family came to America in the 1880's and my mother's family arrived in 1901. 44,000 people were crowded into the North End where only 10,000 + live today. But amazingly there were enclaves of people from the same towns living near each other. My father's family lived in the North Square, Fleet Street area. The predominant town represented here was my father's town Chiusano di San Domenico, Avellino. The Sicilians, especially from the town of Sciacca lived next to them in North Square and on North Street to the end of Fleet Street down to the water. And so it went, the people from certain towns or provinces would be neighbors, living in the same tenement or close by. Many of the immigrants from other towns in the region of Avellino lived on the other side of Hanover Street. The town of my Uncle Tony is a case in point. Most immigrants from Montefalcione (and there were many) lived near or around Sheafe Street. They are famous for the Feast of Saint Anthony in late August.

So, traditions were maintained, food cooked the same way, and the dialect that was spoken could vary from street to street. In my area, some of the Chiusanese Dialect was mixed in with Sicilian. I remember insisting that many words were the correct way of saying something only to realize later that another town had different names for the same items. Welcome to the world of Dialects! We never pronounced the ending syllable of a word. B was the sound for V. Che boi?! We said "ca" instead of "cua", litto instead of letto and never included the last vowel. I thought my mother's first name was Micheli for years, accent on the"li". Grandma never said Michelina. My aunt's last name was Reppucc, not Reppucci, we "ate" the last syllable. I did not know any of these differences until I was older!

And then there were the words that weren't even Italian, but we thought they were. I actually asked for a room with a "Bacahous" (back of the house - outhouse) in a fancy hotel in Rome. One of my friends thought "bolahama" (boiled ham) was an Italian cold cut and he was in college! There were a lot of ways for us to make fools of ourselves outside of the North End.

When meeting a newly arrived immigrant, the first question you ask is where are you from? By the way they spoke you can almost pinpoint the area they are from. But also their answer is never Italy, it is their Town and/or Province they identify with. The Unification of Italy never really united the people in the South to identify as Italians. I will be from Benevento and Chiusano all my life. However, if Italy wins the World Cup, then I am Italian. The whole North End is Italian and all of Massachusetts is Italian!

Churches

So, if you have all these "Italians" you need more churches. The majestic Saint Mary's Jesuit Church on Endicott Street was originally built for the Irish Catholics who had settled in the North End. As the Irish moved out to other parts of Boston, the church's parishioners were replaced by Italians. Saint Mary's Parochial School educated many North End and West End children.

The church was torn down in 1977. It was a very sad time for everyone in the North End, even if it wasn't their church. The decision was never fully explained. However, the destruction of the West End, which was not too far from Saint Mary's did contribute to lowering the numbers of parishioners. In its place stands Casa Maria, Senior Housing. It has a chapel inside that was supposed to have Masses for the residents. I believe now there is a Mass held on Saturday. Fortunately, most residents, can walk to the three other Churches in the North End. But I am still sad when I pass the area.

The destruction of Saint Mary's Church

Saint Leonard's Church is located on the corner of Prince and Hanover Streets. This was my mother's family church and is still mine. The lower Church, Saint Anthony's was opened in

1891 and the upper churches completed in 1899. This church is a Franciscan Church. The Priests spoke Italian as did the Franciscan Brothers and Nuns who staffed the schools in the early days. The church is designed in the Romanesque style and the first church built by Italian immigrants who were also parishioners. My relatives helped build Saint Leonard's, so I have a very strong attachment to this church. At the height of immigration, the church had 20,000 parishioners. Now maybe it has 2000 but growing. The schools are all now condos, except Saint John's, which is the PK-8 elementary school. Saint Anthony's, the lower church, has been turned into the Parish Hall. But Saint Leonard's in all its newly renovated glory still stands proudly, welcoming all to enter through its Peace Garden, which has long taken root on Hanover Street.

Continuing along Hanover Street past Fleet Street is Saint Stephen's Church. It was originally built in 1802–1804 as the New North Church or New North Meeting House and was designed by the architect Charles Bulfinch. In 1862, the Archdiocese bought the church and renamed it St. Stephen's. At this time many Boston Irish attended the church. But again, as the Irish left, newer immigrants would begin to be served at this historic church. My mother was a member of the choir, she was married, I was baptized, and her Funeral Mass was held at Saint Stephen's. I believe a disagreement between my mother and grandmother contributed to my mother changing her church to one across the street from where she lived from one a block away. Lots of choices in the North End.

Off Hanover Street is North Square and there stands Sacred Heart Church. This is the church of my father's family and probably all Chiusanese and most Sicilians. The Seamen's Bethel in Boston was a Methodist Church which later was purchased by the San Marco Society a group of Italian immigrants from Genoa in 1884. Sacred Heart Italian Church was the first church in Boston staffed by the Scalabrini Fathers (since its opening in 1889 until 2004) who came to America to minister to Italian immigrants. In fact, Father Scalabrini was just canonized by Pope Francis this year (2022). The interior of the church is resplendent with brightly painted walls, marble columns and stained-glass windows. Many statues of honored saints reside in front of the church walls and are recipients of a multitude of votive candles, always lit by parishioners for specific intentions. This is an Italian Church! I must add that the same is true of Saint Leonard's. When I enter, I am transported back in time to another era, and I am at peace. It is my heritage, my blood.

Recently, I was at Sacred Heart celebrating the canonization of Father Scalabrini. In a small reception area / kitchen at the back of the Lower Church there were people having coffee and talking and meeting one another. You could see in their faces how happy there were to be in the Church that had been closed for structural reasons almost three years ago, right before Covid hit. Not knowing many people in attendance, I joined a group of people speaking in both Italian and English. I introduced myself and as soon as I did, three women said "I knew your family! You are from Chiusano!" They then proceeded to give me details of many relatives, and they knew so much about my Grandmother Reppucci's side of the family as well. My cousin Stephen came in to meet me, he said "I followed all the noise, and I knew where you would be". He had to keep saying his father was from Northern Italy and he didn't know anything about Chiusano! I don't think I had been as warmly received at any event I have ever attended. People cling fondly to their memories and their provinces and towns with such fervor. To meet another person that shares their roots and heritage is a joy to them and it certainly was to me.

Sacred Heart Church

As we were leaving the coffee area and walking down one of the aisles to exit, I heard someone calling after us. An older man very much in a hurry, was shuffling to catch up to us. We had no idea what he wanted. Finally, he reached us and hugged me! His name is Tony and he spoke in dialect and honestly, I only got part of it, "che cos' felice". He was so happy to meet me and wanted me to visit him and kept hugging me. If someone had seen us, they would think that two long lost friends had just met up again! This to me is the North End! The warm feeling of belonging and people wanting you to belong.

But there existed a bit of friction about what church a family attended. Earlier Italian immigrants went to Sacred Heart as a rule because it was a standing church. While Saint Leonard's Church was opened a year or so later, but only the lower church, the upper church was still being built. Immigrants who had arrived earlier like my father's family went to Sacred Heart and my mother's family who came later went Saint Leonard's. As in any group there was a hierarchy, and in the North End those who immigrated earlier were placed higher up on the social ladder, if a family bought into that status.

Schools

Schools in the North End during my years were mostly Catholic. Elementary schools were Saint Mary's, Saint John's (Part of Sacred Heart) Saint Anthony's, (part of Saint Leonard's), and where I would go for additional lessons and where my mother and all the relatives from her side of the family attended. My cousin Ron still fondly remembers Sister Mary Yolanda who taught Italian.

Beginning in the 1940's there were also two Catholic High Schools, Christopher Columbus for Boys and Julie Billiart for Girls. Both were in the same building but separated into two schools. All my cousins went to these schools.

The North Bennett Industrial School opened in 1881 and was the first vocational school in the country. It was dedicated to helping immigrants acclimate to their new lives. There were many job skill training classes for men and unmarried women and home economics for mothers. My mother went to NBSIS to learn upholstery. When we moved, she upholstered all the living room furniture in our new house. She did a masterful job!

My cousin Angie's story: "My Father's dream had been for me to attend the North Bennet Street School and I did in 1992 when I changed careers and enrolled in the Jewelry Making & Repair Program. After graduating in 1994, the following thirty years have been in the jewelry, watch, clock, and luxury goods businesses. I became a Graduate Gemologist, GIA and a Certified Gemologist, AGS. In addition to my own services as a jeweler, gemologist and estate evaluator, I have been employed by two highly regarded jewelry companies in Boston, Shreve, Crump & Lowe and Tiffany & Co. I have North Bennett Street School to thank for my success."

The North Bennett Street School as it exists today offers classes in at least nine trades and fine crafts.

There were elementary public schools in the North End as well and my mother would threaten to send me to the 'Protestant School" if I misbehaved. That threat worked and turned me into an angelic child, at least temporarily.

In retrospect, I think the education that the boys at Christopher Columbus High School received was very good. They were taught by the Franciscan Priests and Brothers. My cousins and many friends went on to college and graduate school. But the girls were not going to college at the same rate as the boys were. I went to an all-girls Catholic School outside the North End and we all went to college upon graduating. I believe the Italian cultural norm of girls just needing to get a job and find a husband was still prevalent in the North End, even in the 60's. My parents never thought this way.

Saint Anthony's School on North Bennett Street - 1907

Shops and More Shops

Salem Street was the place to buy anything you needed. During my younger years, although most of the Jewish population had moved to other parts of Boston or to cities close by, there were still Jewish owned stores, mainly dry goods doing business on Salem Street.

Clayman's was my favorite, you could get anything you needed there: linens, fabric, clothes, dolls, Christening dresses. It was amazing array, and you could put a little money toward whatever you wanted each week. I remember my aunt always doing this for tablecloths. Italians loved tablecloths! Of course, you also put plastic over them so they wouldn't get stained.

Right near Clayman's was "The Saint Store" for saint statues or pictures or rosary beads or votive candles or saint medals, all your basic Italian Catholic necessities. We always went in to look and usually bought at least one item, even if it was just a prayer card. I called them Holy Cards.

Clayman's

Then there was the food! Many meat shops, fish markets, and vegetable and fruit stores lined Salem Street with produce in baskets and crates also on the sidewalks as well as inside. There were also the pushcart vendors selling their specific food in the street which was also jammed with trucks and cars. No one just meandered down Salem Street, you quickly learned to plot a path to your destinations. My favorite pushcart was Quahog Man. We always bought quahogs fresh on Friday mornings as we ate stuffed quahogs every Friday night. Quahog Man knew us, and he knew my mother always had to select the quahogs herself. They were strewn across ice shavings in the pushcart and Mama would inspect them all carefully before she would point to the six that she thought were the best to be had. Mama had Quahog Man charmed.

Salem Street - 1950's (Photo: Courtesy of Vito Aluia)

We had a set route. Every Friday we would walk down Parmenter Street, go left on Salem Street and left down the tiny stairs into Silvio's Vegetable and Fruit store. He was also a Bookie, so Mama handed him a lot of small pieces of papers. Then across the street to Pat the Butcher. He knew everything my mother wanted and Tudi would cut everything to order. The humongous cleaver scared me to death as he chopped away on the large wooden butcher block table that was firmly positioned on the sawdust covered wood floor. Then naturally, the quahogs and fish were last. And if you are a North Ender you have to remember the snails that would be inching their way up their silver cylindrical container outside of Giuffre's Fish Market on the corner of Salem and Cross Street!

After we walked home and placed all the food where it belonged in my Nonna's flat and in ours. we quickly crossed the street to Iacopucci's. This was time to buy the salami, mortadella, capicola, provolone, all sliced just the way Mama liked it and wrapped individually with the transparent paper and then all wrapped again with butcher paper and sealed. She would buy the mozzarella, sold separately in oval balls, black olives, and pepperoncini. Tonno/tuna and anchovies, both packed in olive oil and in tin cans which were hard to open, were also on our order, The anchovies' tin even had a key! The best part was the tuna sandwiches, huge and scrumptious. It was Friday and we couldn't eat meat, so all the cold cuts were for Saturday and the rest of the week. By the time we were finished we left with two or more shopping bags, more sore hands and our mouths were watering, waiting to eat tuna sandwiches.

Salem and Parmenter Streets

SOCIETIES:
Social and Saintly

Just as in Italy, there were many societies in the North End. These societies could be social/civic clubs and/or religious societies. Many saints had their own societies, and they were celebrated on their feast days in church and some also with parades, better known as feasts. Although 50 individual religious societies once existed in the North End only 12 remain today. Two of the most notable societies are San Antonio Di Padova Da Montefalcione Society and The Fisherman's Society – Madonna Del Soccorso di Sciacca Society. These societies sponsor and organize the two largest feasts which take place each August. They have changed over the years, but I can still remember the thrill when Saint Anthony passed by carried by Society Members.

Societies with their religious Feasts have a place in my heart. I remember pleading with my mother to be the angel who flies across the street at the Fisherman's Feast on North Street, just down a block from our flat on Fleet Street. Mama kept saying "No" and I kept asking and asking! Finally, one day she said "when you become Sicilian I will ask the Society". And, as we say, that ended that dream!

The Fisherman's Feast has been held in the North End since 1910, a tradition brought here by the Sicilian town of Sciacca. This town has a passionate devotion to the Madonna del Soccorso. The Feast is run by the original descendants of the immigrants from Sciacca. The feast ends with "the Flight of the Angel".

Saint Anthony Feast Decorations

Chapter 3

Grandma Nonna

Grandma stomped or shuffled into a room, depending on her mood. She was 4'10" of pure Neapolitan attitude with jet black hair that was always in a bun at the nape of her neck, eyes of coal that would turn cloudy with age and always dressed in black. Grandma would never be called a Nonna that was calm and meek, most of the time she would be a roll of thunder or a bolt of lightning. She never spoke English, but she could read and write in Italian. Maybe it was her stature, becoming a widow at an early age or losing a child, or just having to survive in a strange country with two young daughters or a combination of all she had endured, but she was a force to be reckoned with.

But there was another side of Grandma. On her bedroom dresser, next to all the pictures, statues of Saints and Rosary Beads dangling from the dresser mirror, stood at least three clocks. None were electric. But why three, maybe four? She was a member of the Third Order of Saint Francis. I'm not sure if it was a requirement of the Third Order, but she went to Mass everyday. Not just one, all of them. An alarm clock would ring to signal a time to leave and off she'd trudge across Hannover Street (the main street in the North End) to Saint Leonard's, to the downstairs church called Saint Anthony's for Masses at 6 a.m., 8 a.m., 10 a.m. and maybe noon. I don't quite remember the schedule. Most days, I would be sitting beside my grandmother in the pew as she whispered her prayers in Italian, hunched over in submission to a higher power that she believed in so ardently. There was no messing around with Grandma at church, I sat there quietly, and then I got to light candles in the Grotto. The Grotto was my favorite place. It was in the back of the church and the entrance was down a step. The walls were made of large stones, creating a replica of a grotto. When I entered, directly in front of me was a large statue of the Pieta, the statue of Mary holding Jesus when He was taken down from the cross. Other Saints' statues were vying for attention, but the

Pieta was the centerpiece of the Grotto and always had the most candles lit. Lighting candles cost money, so this was a huge deal as grandma did not easily part with money.

```
TERZ'ORDINE DI SAN FRANCESCO D'ASSISI
      Provincia dell' Immacolata Concezione
              New York, N. Y.

Fratello  ⎱  Vincenza Toto
Sorella   ⎰
Indirizzo......19 Fleet St. Boston, Mass.
Data di Recezione......May 5, 1918
Data di Professione......June 8, 1919
Chiesa......St. Leonard's
Città......Boston......Stato......Mass.
Direttore......Fr Benjamin O.F.M.
Data......August 24, 1953
```

Vincenza Iuliucci was born on June 6, 1881 in Airola a small town near Benevento the provincial capital in the region of Campania, the capital of which is Naples. In 1901, she and her two sisters, Mariuccia and Antonetta and her parents embarked on the journey to America out of the port of Naples and landed in Ellis Island. I am not sure how they came to live in the North End, but I suspect a family member was already there.

In 1909 she married my grandfather, Michele Toto who hailed from Lacedonia, Avellino. The ceremony was held at Saint Leonard's Church. This is the grandest church in the North End and built by Italian Immigrants. Grandma soon had two daughters, Angelina who died as an infant and my Aunt Assunta. Sadly, Angelina was never mentioned, and I only learned about this tragedy from my mother, after my grandmother had passed.

My Grandfather's Town - Lacedonia

In 1911, my grandfather was discovered to have Tuberculosis and was sent back to Italy where the temperate climate would help his failing health. My distraught grandmother, who was again pregnant and my aunt, who was a toddler, followed my grandfather to Italy shortly after he had departed in 1911. Other family members also returned to Italy to be of comfort to my grandmother. As the story was passed down to me, my mother, Michelina, was born two days after my grandfather died. Soon after, World War 1 broke out and Grandma and her two daughters were stranded in Italy until it was safe to travel. When they returned to the North End, they had no money, no clothes, nothing. They were on relief, as aid for the poor was called back then and lived in a two-room cold water flat. By the time my mother was 8 she was working at my Great Uncle's butcher shop in North Square. She would be assigned the jobs no one wanted. She swept the sawdust off the grimy floor and took the refuse to the back alley. Rats enjoyed coming out to greet my mother! They had taken up residence in the alleys of the North End in the 1920's as they could easily find food to eat. My Aunt Assunta who had heart problems, never worked. Grandma somehow summoned the strength to hold this small family together. Many would have failed but my Nonna was not just anyone, she was as tough as nails.

My Mother and Aunt

When my mother was married in 1935, she moved into my father's family house, which he now owned. This was a huge climb up on the North End Social Ladder for my mother. And my Grandma came too and climbed up to the top floor to her very own flat! It was a package deal. The North End tenements were overcrowded small "cold water flats" sometimes two flats to a floor with a toilet in the hallway for all that floor's residents to utilize. Tenements were brick buildings of various levels and outer ornamentation. My father's was four levels, with simple ornamentation, built in 1893. The first floor was a bakery, second floor was our apartment, third floor was rented out and

Grandma had the fourth floor. By the time I was born in 1949 our flat was a "real" apartment with central heat, an inside bathroom, a "modern kitchen" including a refrigerator, a white enamel gas stove, hot water and even a breakfast nook. There

was also a living room with a fake brick fireplace and two bedrooms. The top two floors were a bit smaller, but still had two larger rooms and two small bedrooms. Ahhh, but entering my grandma's was a big step back in time, way back to 1893!

Grandma was not big on change, she wanted nothing replaced or tampered with. Although she did have electricity, it was hardly used and the ice man came up the three flights of wooden stairs to fortify her not one, but two iceboxes, one cream colored and one light green. Grandma didn't believe in throwing things out. A huge cast iron black coal stove occupied the opposite wall from the two iceboxes. A good sized white enameled sink with one faucet decorated the back wall and the front of the kitchen had two windows that looked out to the street far below. Fire escapes were outside each window.

The kitchen table that stood between the two windows was a large brown enamel bulky affair which was the gathering spot and center of all activity. All food preparation, meals, and conversations between family and friends were at the table. She also would sew and crochet at the table, always making sure it was spotless and no-one came near her. Grandma was an incredibly talented crocheter. From bed linens, to doilies to the popcorn crocheted bedspread, her creations were widely praised. I still have them! There was no living room. What would have been the living room was my Nonna's bedroom. There was a door to another room (I was never sure) off her bedroom but there was a vanity in front of it blocking the entrance. The other small bedroom that was entered from the kitchen, had a

Nonna's Crochet Work

day bed which was where I slept. Everything in there smelled of mothballs. And yes, the toilet with the pull chain was in the hallway.

As it was the hub of all activity, Grandma and I spent most of our time in the kitchen, when we weren't in church or haggling with the vegetable man for a cheaper price for tomatoes and peppers. Most nonne cooked, mine did not. She ate with us, my mother being the best cook in the world. Grandma's one and only specialty was peppers and eggs and coffee. Coffee was consumed morning, noon and night and some might say it was sugar with a little coffee added. This is why I became a tea drinker and never use sugar. The only meat I ever saw in the flat were sausages and those might have gone into the pepper and egg mixture. When we ate sandwiches from Iacopucci's grocery store it was a huge deal! I would cross Fleet Street and Mario, the owner's super handsome son, would make up cold cut sandwiches. I even got a coke from the enamel beverage chest that contained the blocks of ice that kept everything inside nice and cold. These incredible sandwiches can never be duplicated ask anyone in the North End. But despite the lack of luxury, there was lots of love for each other and we enjoyed our times together. But we did get into some trouble.

As I got a bit older, my Nonna took me to places I had never been, the first I remember was the Prado. I had to hold her hand at all times and I struggled to keep up with her as she plowed through the crowded streets as if she were a midwife rushing to deliver a baby. The Prado was a park entered on Hanover Street in between Saint Stephen's Church and The Old North Church. At the entrance was a huge statue of Paul Revere on his horse. I always wanted to climb up on that horse. North Enders loved to gather there to talk, and the men would play card games. There were lots of pigeons and I could actually run around. When I saw the candy store I begged and begged to go inside. Only once in all our visits did she let me go in and buy some candy. It was a special treat. We never had candy, as my mother's cooking talents extended to baking cookies, pies and cakes of all kinds.

Yes, We Have No Bananas

But the day we went to Haymarket was truly memorable. I was maybe 5 or 6. I thought we were going to buy a lot of fruits and vegetables. But my grandma was in search of only one specific item, crates, as many as the two of us could carry. Back at her kitchen, I then was taught the art of carpentry and demolition. With hammers we got the nails out of the crates, broke the wood in half and piled the pieces of wood, in a box next to the stove. This was hard work and I got a lot of splinters and banged my fingers a few times as well. Next, the wood from the box was placed into the black coal stove and lit to create the fire to heat the flat, cook the food and make the coffee (this step she did not allow me to do). My Grandma saved money where she could and coal cost money. All was going smoothly until my mother came home from work and saw me on the floor with hammer in hand. My mother excelled at yelling and so did Nonna! But Mama won and I was never to touch another hammer. But the trouble didn't end here.

HOT TOWN, SUMMER IN THE CITY

Summers were hot in the North End. Tenements rarely had cross air ventilation. But to escape the heat we had fire escapes, and it wasn't unusual for people to sleep outside on them all night. My favorite spot was the fire escape outside the window in my little room in my Nonna's flat. I would have a blanket and a pillow and play with my stuffed animal Winkie. Even in the mid afternoon under a blazing sun, it was better than being inside without any air. I could also see the kids racing their home-made scooters made out of crates along the street. I had a bird's eye view of the hustle and bustle of people going into my favorite stores, Iacopucci's Italian Groceries and my aunt's florist shop. I was maybe six at the time. When my mother came home from work, this particular day was steaming and so was my mother. She was screeching at my grandmother, asking where I was, and was told I was outside on the fire escape. My mother ran into the tiny bedroom and reached out the window and grabbed me by my pig tails and pulled me inside the bedroom. She was breathing so hard she couldn't talk. When she caught her breath the yelling started and my grandmother was the recipient of a litany of Italian curses, another talent my mother had. This was worse than the day of the crate adventure. All I could understand was "dangerous", as the high pitch yelling continued. I had never seen my mother and grandma so mad at each other. Finally, my mother reminded my grandma that all the fire escapes in the building had been condemned by the City and needed to be repaired. Apparently my Nonna forgot this important fact. My mother then added, a young child like me should never be out on the fire escape in the first place. Grandma actually apologized to my mother, and that all the kids were always on the fire escapes, but she didn't realize that it was unsafe. Two major events occurred that day; one, my grandmother apologizing to my mother and second, the last time I was allowed on a fire escape. My head hurt for at least two days as my hair was almost pulled out of my scalp. But as time went on things would change.

Water Please

My Nonna only spoke in Neapolitan Dialect with a bit of Sicilian thrown in for added flavor! So for the sixteen and a half years we spent together, that was the "Italian" I knew. It was what my mother, my father, and all the relatives spoke. If it wasn't exactly the same, it was pretty close. I think that is why we love singing, because all the best Italian songs are from Napoli and most words are in Dialect. As I was always with Grandma she would ask me favors: help wash the floor, go across the street to Iacopucci's and even the menial tasks of getting her some water, coffee or wine. I was at her beck and call, she was Grandma Nonna! So frequently, she would say to me "Da me pechile dacqu' ". I thought that was, get me a little water and I did. Now Italians are known for their hand gestures and Grandma was no exception. After she drank, she would have her hand outstretched and her thumb pointing downward, and she would say "naboge". I figured that meant "some more". Now this started when I was about three years old. Apparently we had our own dialect called "Third Floor, Fleet Street". And through the years the "Dialect" was expanded and refined. Frankly, I am surprised that we weren't offered a book deal to write a dictionary.

But I need to mention what: "Da me pechile dacqu' " really means, And "naboge", well, I still have no clue what that means! Probably "Grandma Sign Language" means the same thing! What ever she wanted to drink, she wanted it now. All of these happy Nonna memories were triggered by the fact that yesterday, while watching Don Mateo (an Italian TV program), I heard the "Italian" word for glass, bicchiere. Phonetically in English that would be, be key - air- re, with the last three sylables all blended. A light bulb went on in my head, and I thought, could "pechile" mean "Glass" to Nonna? I immediately called my good friends and neighbors Irma and Mike. Mike is from Basilicata. He speaks his own dialect but close enough to where we are from to help decipher the mystery word of the day. He corroborated that grandma's word was indeed dialect for the "Italian bicchiere" word. She probably never knew the

"Italian word' and I didn't make the connection until yesterday that pechile didn't me small!

What does this mean to me? True love has its own language. Non ti dimenticherò mai! I love you, 'a voglio bene assaje, Grandma Nonna.

My House Today, 19 Fleet Street, North End 02113

The Frame Up

Grandma appeared to be this gentle, kind and quiet Nonna and my friends all remember her with warm regard. But Grandma could be devious. She'd hide contraband! When she was sick and living with us, she fortunately recuperated with the seemingly endless and exhausting nursing care of my mother. Grandma then got her own bedroom upstairs. She was cautioned "please, no food allowed in your bedroom". Cleaning every week revealed stashes of mints and Ritz Crackers. The edict would be repeated, but to no avail. And she used the age-old excuse, "They aren't mine and I don't know how they got up here", but in dialect "No sace' da dove ha venati". One day I came home from school and my mother quickly called me into the kitchen. Grandma was sitting at the kitchen table, all smiles. Mama was not smiling and turned to me holding pieces of a broken, very old small Deruta vase! "Why did I find these in your jean pockets when I was doing the wash?" She was interrogating me as if she were Sergeant Joe Friday on Dragnet. I boldly replied, "I never did this, I never broke anything"!

This small vase was brought to America from Italy by my family in 1901, along with other Deruta China. Grandma is sitting there quietly and Mama is still waiting for a full confession. I was not going to take the blame for something I did not do, but how did the pieces all get in my jean pockets? Mama may have thought she was Joe Friday, but I knew I WAS Nancy Drew and I would get to the bottom of this crime. Following the deductive procedures of Nancy Drew, I deduced Grandma had set me up. There were three of these vases on a shelf going upstairs. Now there were two and the broken one found in my pockets. I don't think Daddy ever went upstairs. So that left Grandma as the only possible culprit. Looking back I always felt bad about this. I should have realized Grandma was afraid. She thought perhaps Mama would get so mad, she would tell her to leave, because of the broken vase and the mints and the crackers. I do have to applaud Grandma's shrewd skills at framing me for the incident though. The next time she broke anything, I told her I would cover for her. Mama can't throw me out.

Two Remaining Vases

Deruta Pottery: Tea Pot, Creamer and Sugar Bowl. Part of the set my Family brought with them from Italy - 1901

Nonna was getting old, too old and wasn't taking care of herself properly. She caught pneumonia and came to live with us in our new house. She regained her strength but through the whole time living with us, she couldn't go to church, or haggle with the vegetable man or carry the crates back to her kitchen. I was older and she didn't have to take care of me. She was depressed and hardly talked. Mumbling the Rosary, she sat in what I called "grandma's chair" and would stare and stare. I bet she was thinking of her life story, her country, her husband, her infant daughter, her journey and how happy she was in her 1893 flat that had never changed. We were all sad and worried that Grandma would slip away. We had sold our house in the North End, so she couldn't go back there. But my mother came up with the idea of Nonna returning to the North End to another flat. Miraculously, she found an updated flat owned by the Reppuccis on Garden Court Street just around the corner from our old building. Grandma was so excited, her face grew brighter, she started talking to us, she ate all her dinner, even yelled sometimes, she stomped when she walked, and you could even hear her sing! She would be able to go to her church! Nonna was going back home.

Nonna in "Grandma's Chair"

Grandma Nonna, Mama and Auntie Susie - 1917

*Mama about 1930
Marcell Hair*

Chapter 4

Michelina Angelina
My Mama

My mother was born two days after my grandfather died. I do not know if her birth created any joy to my now widowed grandmother. What I do know is that Mama made her entrance into the chaotic world of pre-World War 1 Italy.

Nonna immigrated to the North End of Boston from a small town near Benevento, Italy, with her two sisters and mother and father in 1901. She married my grandfather in 1909. He was much younger than her. This was a common occurrence as getting married for a girl was the chief objective, not what age anyone was. She quickly had two babies, Angelina and Assunta. Infant death was an unwelcomed visitor in this era and Angelina died shortly after birth. When my grandfather was sent back to Italy after he was diagnosed with Tuberculosis, Nonna, again pregnant, and toddler Assunta followed him. In 1917, my Nonna and my Aunt Assunta would travel back to America along with the additional bundle, my mother.

My Mother

And so the story of Michelina Angelina begins in Boston's North End. The family having no assets, somehow found a two room flat across from Saint Stephen's Church. My mother shared many stories from these very hard times, living in poverty, despair and a constant fear of becoming homeless.

There wasn't much to eat, although my Nonna's sister's husband, Uncle Pasquale, had a meat market in North Square. So in order to get some food my mother at the age of 8 began working there at my Uncle's insistence: "no free food, you have to work for it". My Great Aunt Mariuccia would sneak some food to her sister and two nieces, but the constant fear of abuse by her husband limited her ability to help. Domestic abuse was never talked about but was common. Even their daughter, my much-loved Auntie Anna told her family that she had grown up with an abusive father. Unfortunately, my mother saw abuse at a young age and perhaps she just accepted this brutality as part of the life of being a woman. It was ingrained in her.

Trip To the Relief Station

This small, destitute family was on Relief, as assistance to the poor was called at that time. There was a Relief Station in Haymarket Square. Food was doled out on certain days to those "on the dole". My grandmother could not leave her two young girls alone. My Aunt had heart problems and was mostly confined to the flat, so my mother was the one sent to Haymarket to get what meager food was being given. One wintry day my mother had to go to the relief station and get the food. Her total wardrobe consisted of a tattered, thread bare dress, jacket, stockings, and scarf which doubled as a hat as warranted. All were hand me downs from my aunt who was 3 years older and very tall. And these items were hand me downs to my aunt by the Relief Station. Shoes were a big problem as my aunt had small feet and by the time my mother got them there were still way too small for Mama's larger feet and she has blisters all the time from trying to squish her feet inside them. In addition, the shoes had many holes in the soles and newspaper was put inside the shoes to cover the holes, but did not keep out the cold, rain or snow. Wearing this unsuitable outfit she went out on the slippery, snow ladened cobblestone streets of Boston's North End, the wind at her back. Once at the relief station she had to wait in a long line. When it was her turn, she was given just two eggs, that was all. She turned toward home and this time the wind was not at her back but coming straight at her. The snow-covered street had turned to ice, she slipped and fell and the precious eggs were broken. When she arrived home, she was shivering, her clothing all wet and with tears in her eyes told Grandma what had occurred. Poor Mama was slapped in the face and cursed as this was the only food they had and how could she be so clumsy.

Surprisingly, Mama was able to attend school! When she arrived from Italy, she first went to kindergarten. Her young teacher was Bertha K. Rice. She loved my mother. Realizing her impoverished life, Miss Rice would be extra kind to her. Miss Rice gave Mama a miniature green china tea set which Mama treasured and I still have! My mother always corresponded with Miss Rice and often sent her gifts. Miss Rice outlived my mother and sent a very consoling card and letter to me when she learned of my mother's passing.

Miss Rice's Thoughtful Gift! 1917

Mama then attended grammar school with the Italian speaking Franciscan Sisters at Saint Anthony's School, the Parish School of Saint Leonard's Church. She still worked after school at Uncle Pasquale's meat market. As she got older, in 7th grade she began working at H.P. Hood. When she graduated 8th grade, she could not advance in school as she was the sole support of her family. From graduation on, she was employed full time by H. P. Hood. She worked there for several years and even got an award and medal when she left. Most girls did not continue to high school in the 1920's. In fact, girls were married very young and many were arranged marriages for economic reasons. It was not uncommon for a girl to get married at 14 years of age. But my mother was needed at home, so marriage fortunately was not an option.

Kindergarten picture: 1917 when Mama arrived from Italy

Because my mother was working and helping her mother and sister survive, she now also had money of her own. Mama had a big heart and loved animals. Someone gave her three Spitz dogs (now called American Eskimo dogs) and she had a cat named Kitty Boy. She had to feed and take care of all of them! How did the family of three and all these animals fit in this two-room flat? But Mama made it work and now had time to spend with her cousin Anna and friends she had from work.

And young men entered her life. Mama was beautiful and even if she had only one good dress to wear when she went out, she always turned the young men's heads. She would be "courted" by many!

Mama left behind a lot of pictures. Her group of friends would go horseback riding, ice skating and dancing. They would go to the Totem Pole in Norumbega Park to dance. The "girlfriends" even rented a cottage in New Hampshire! That amazed me! But all the "fun" was away from the North End.

She was a bridesmaid and godmother for many members of her family My Godmother, Auntie Jennie would tell me everyone chose her for a godmother because she gave really nice gifts! Mama was kindhearted, and a giver. Mama's life was getting better, and not plagued with the drudgery and misery of when she was younger. She had a radiant smile in all her pictures. But as I reflect on her life, I am not sure if this happiness was also in her soul.

In October of 1935, Mama was 23 years old, and she married my father Joseph Fucillo who was 14 years her senior. She was very close to his family and my father's niece Esther, was my mother's Maid of Honor. The North End is very small geographically and it becomes smaller when you are looking for a wife or husband. In my opinion this marriage was a win win for both my mother and father. My mother was looking for stability and my father was looking for someone young and beautiful. I really would like to think love was involved as well. Mama had a big wedding and it was a very social affair. My father was Governor Curley's Chauffeur and a state trooper and a lot of state dignitaries attended. Mary Curley the Governor's daughter attended the wedding as she and my mother had become good friends. Mama and Daddy went to Bermuda for their honeymoon. Mama hit the North End Social Jackpot. She moved into the house my father's family had owned, which was now my father's. She finally had a

home; she got to decorate, entertain, wear gorgeous clothes and be the beautiful woman by the side of my father. Most importantly, she had the stability that my father offered her. The Fucillos had lived an immigrant life so different from my mother. Imagine, a father who worked hard and bought a whole tenement house, who had four sons who had made something of themselves and also had homes and families. I wonder if my mother felt out of place in such an atmosphere. But she was elegant and graceful, and no one could tell that her family was "on the dole", without anything to call their own, little food and clothes, and no father to care for them.

She was called "Mrs. Joseph Fucillo, pretty North End matron of 19 Fleet Street" in a Globe newspaper article.

But how did she cope with my father's interest in running for political office and not being home as much as she would have liked?

I do not know when the marriage began to fall apart. But my parents were unable to have a child for a long time and my father's political ambitions failed as political appointments and status declined. Although not a heavy drinker at all, he would lash out when he did drink, even a little. My mother was the recipient of this behavior. But the good news was that I was born! It brought them together, but that did not last very long and they soon separated. My mother filed for divorce, which was unheard of at the time. But the divorce went through quickly. My  mother and I were in the flat and she still had her friends over to see me toddle around and celebrate my birthdays. But she needed the stability she had lost when she and my father divorced.

My Mother and me. 1949

She soon met an attractive man, and they were married within a short period of time. Sadly, history repeated itself, as he was older, in politics and he liked to drink. After their marriage, my mother and I and now, my second father moved into a beautiful 2 family house out of the North End, leaving my grandmother on the top floor of the tenement. We were in the North End at least three times a week to visit grandma and other relatives and do the food shopping. My mother would clean Nonna's flat, buy her food and cook for her. Every Wednesday on her hands and knees with a scrub brush and buckets of water, Mama would wash down tenement stairs. On Sundays Grandma came to our house. Our ties to the North End were never broken.

This second marriage, although love was certainly a component, was filled with fights and abuse due to alcohol and my mother's inherent psychological issues that would exacerbate problems instead of calming them. Tragically, my mother attempted suicide three times, that I know of. When I was 15 in 1964, my second father was diagnosed with Cirrhosis and died in 1966. These two remaining years were probably the best years of their marriage. But now my mother was alone again and without my father's income. She still worked and had her card club on Saturdays with friends from the West End: sisters Rose, Josie, Anne and some others from the North End.

But she was never the same. Mama began to sell items in our home. Once I had graduated from college and working, I was frequently home and gave her money each month. In fact, those were our best times together. In May of 1976 she was misdiagnosed with TB and then correctly diagnosed with cancer. In only five months Mama died a horrible death, ten years after my second father died. My beautiful mother, with the perpetual, captivating smile and engaging personality on the outside, had been emotionally dying inside all her life. Her life as an immigrant was traumatic. These experiences created anxiety, depression and fear of abandonment, abuse, and poverty, that would haunt her all her life. A life, that at times, she wanted to end.

Chapter 5

My Daddy Joe

I called my father Daddy Joe. His family was from Chiusano di San Domenico, Avellino. Daddy's father Teodoro immigrated first in 1881 and his brothers, Louis, Ralph and John and his mother Josephine arrived a bit later. Four out of seven children survived. I have no clue as to why Uncle Ralph settled in Rockland, as did Uncle John. But I have great stories. My father was the last son born very late to my grandparents, and he was the only family member born in the United States. He was born in Boston in 1898. His name on his Baptism Record was Generoso, but somehow was changed to Joseph. None of the family was formally educated, either in Italy or Massachusetts. But all spoke Italian and in time, all four sons could read and write English as well as Italian. All of the family anglicized their names, which makes it difficult to find records. Also writing on many documents was difficult to decipher, and written haphazardly by officials. I would find Fuccillo written as Fucillo, Iucillo, Tucillo or other misspellings in my research. But the true name is Fuccillo. How do I know? It is on the Gravestones! No one made mistakes on Italian gravestones.

Regardless, this Fucillo family did well when they arrived in Massachusetts and achieved the immigrant dream. Uncle John became the Chief of Police in Rockland and even married an "American" (actually from Nova Scotia). My mother really liked Theresa and once whispered to me, "she's American, you know". Their descendants are still in the Rockland area as are Uncle Ralph's who worked as a laborer and then for the town as a plumber and ultimately Water Commissioner. Uncle Louis lived in the North End and when he got married, he moved to Chelsea to a very lovely two-family home on Garfield Avenue. As they were the closest geographically, we visited them often. Uncle Louis and his wife, Zia Michelina (Cataldo) were blessed to have five children: Josephine, Esther, Theodore, Armando and Eva and sadly one child, Umberto Teodoro who died at 8 months of whopping cough. Technically, they were my first cousins, but they were my mother's age, so they were my aunts and uncles. Uncle Armando was my Godfather.

Brotherly Love - In the Still of the Night

My father's older brother John was the Chief of Police in Rockland. I have no idea, how this Italian immigrant coming to this country as a young man became the Chief of Police, but he did. His name was frequently in the newspaper. This was during the 1920's, the time of Prohibition. If a still was discovered, owners and workers were arrested, the still shut down, and the liquor confiscated. My uncle was very busy, as Rockland apparently was a prime area for stills. I heard this all from my mother and as I looked up news-paper stories, all she told me was verified. However, there was one part missing. I found a couple of other articles. One night on April 28 of 1925 my father was arrested on a charge of unlawfully transporting intoxicating liquor. However, the Globe printed a retraction in the morning edition the following day, stating my father "was not arrested for transporting rum and not engaged in transporting that commodity." I will always wonder what exactly, if anything, these two bothers might have been conspiring.

My father in the 1920's

As I mentioned, Daddy married Mama in 1935 and were quite content living on Fleet Street, the family home of my grandparents, Theodore and Josephine Fucillo. When my grandfather passed my father inherited the building. My grandmother Josephine suffered a long illness and my mother had nursed her daily. She died in 1936. In the tenements of the North End and in Italian family culture, parents and grandparents usually lived with or near their children and were cared by them in their older years. My mother's mother, Grandma Nonna Vincenza now lived in the tenement as well. Therefore, married life got off to a sad start, but my father was quite busy with his duties for Governor James Michael Curley.

My Aunt Esther was Maid of Honor. My father's three brothers and my Uncle Tony is pictured at the far right.

Get Me To The Church On Time

One of these important duties was on a Sunday, my Uncle Tony's car had broken down and it was the Baptism Day of my cousin Baby Tony. My Uncle panicked as he had no way to get my Aunt Anna and Baby Tony to Saint Leonard's in time for the Baptism. Thinking quickly, he called his friend Joe and asked if he could drive them to the church. Well my father showed up in the Governor's Limousine, License Plate S1, and sped through the recently opened East Boston tunnel and into the North End in record time and arrived just as the Church bells of Saint Leonard's were chiming. The funniest part of the story was the look on the toll taker's face as the limousine whizzed by, as he expected to wave to the governor and instead saw a baby in a baptismal gown in my aunt's arms. My father had saved the day!

The marriage seemed to be crumbling, my father was not working as much for the state or city as he once was, but my parents had me! They waited a long time before I came along.

They were so happy again. However, the joy of having me wore off in time, and the marriage soon failed.

Here is where mother's insecurities came into play, as she always insisted I be on my best behavior when visiting the Fucillos. They were the "haves", and she was the "have not". But even though she had divorced my father, they would say she didn't divorce them, and we would always be Family. In retrospect, the Fucillos knew the problems my mother had faced and never blamed her. When we visited, I was dressed in Sunday best and didn't talk much. I smiled a lot and loved all the food Auntie Josie put in from of me. They also gave me a lot of gifts and a fashionable dress when I was in my first year of college! Our family had a lot of Josephines because our grandmother's name was Josephine, she anglicized it from Giusippina when they came to America. If you know or meet a Josephine Fucillo they are connected to my family, and my middle name is Josephine. Theodore Fucillo, my grandfather had a lot of the boys in his family named after him. If you meet a Theodore Fucillo, he is probably somehow related to me as well. It is the Italian way. The tradition is to name after a grandparent and sometimes one that had passed, to honor the family.

A few years after my mother divorced and remarried, we left the North End. But my father would still see me. However, my mother and I would always meet him in the dingy, smelly MTA Station at the Old State House. He and I would hug and kiss and talk and he would give me presents. Regrettably that is all I can remember. As I write this, I think of how sad that was and fill up with tears. I do have one memory of Daddy Joe asking my mother if we could go and see a movie, "Around the World in 80 Days". My mother said we didn't have time and she and I took the train back home.

I treasured his gifts. I still have them, well almost. I have a pretty pink pocketbook which closed with a fashionable clasp and had a sophisticated strap. It was also a music box! At the beginning of the school year, he gave me a huge set of colored pencils. I couldn't wait to bring them to school the next day to show them off to my classmates. For Christmas when I was in the second grade, he gave me a huge gift! A sage green Smith Corona typewriter! My mother thought it was a ridiculous gift as I was only in second grade. But I proved her wrong and started typing that very night! When my daughter was small, I had the typewriter totally refurbished and one year it was her Christmas gift as well. She also started typing that very day! I also received a pink Bunny Rabbit as a gift one Easter, that was also music box. It came from the Boston Music Company on Boylston Street. That pink Bunny Rabbit was so important to me, a connection to my father and I always carried it with me around the house.

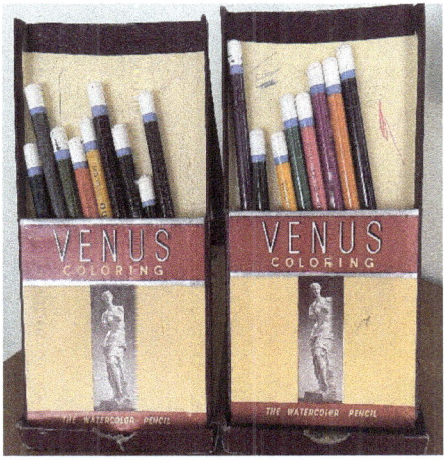

One day I came home from school and my Bunny Rabbit was not on top of the Piano with the rest of the Easter decorations. I ran to my mother and asked where it was. She told me her friend from work had come to visit with her little girl. They were refugees from Hungary and the little girl had nothing, just the clothes on her back. My mother offered to help the family, with clothes and toys and also gave her my Bunny Rabbit. I think Mama honestly forgot it was from Daddy Joe. But I can remember how much I cried and cried that she would give Daddy Joe's Bunny away. Such a vivid traumatic memory, I really was hysterical. I don't know how long I cried but it was a long time. I am not sure when, but soon after my mother bought the same Bunny at the Boston Music Company to make up for her unintentional mistake. I still

have Bunny and it plays music. The music to remember my Daddy Joe, who I would meet at the MTA station.

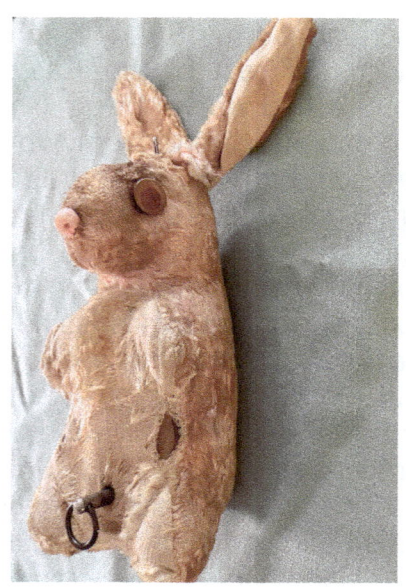

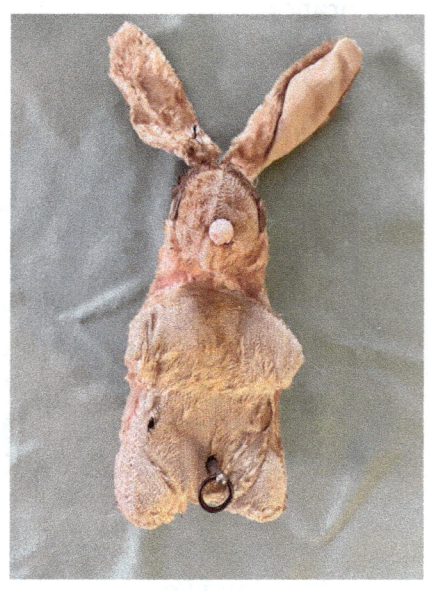

There came a time when I was in fifth grade that I realized my father was sick, really sick. I imagine my mother told me. My second father, Daddy Gene, would drive us all to Carney Hospital on Sundays. My mother would get out of the car and go visit Daddy Joe. Children were not allowed to visit, so I stayed in the car in silence until my mother returned. One Sunday we didn't go to visit the hospital. My father had died. Daddy Joe had died of stomach cancer.

He was buried in Holy Cross Cemetery, alongside his mother and father. I never attended the burial. But Italians visit cemeteries a lot. My Daddy Gene would take Mama and me to the cemetery to put flowers on Daddy Joe's grave and my Grandparents' graves numerous times throughout the year.

Daddy Joe had a loving successful family. Although he was never formally educated, he could read and write in both Italian and English. He was a barber and his nickname was Joe the Barber. It seemed like every guy in the North End had a nickname! He was also a boxer and fought in the Boston Arena. And he owned a restaurant for a time, I still have the dinner plates.

Dinner Plate from Daddy Joe's Restaurant

He worked for Governor James Michael Curley and was appointed head of various state commissions. He unsuccessfully ran for State Senator, one of the first Italians to do so. He owned his own home. He had a beautiful wife who supported him, but the marriage failed. And then he succumbed to cancer, at only 60 years old.

I remember my Daddy Joe from pictures, meetings in an MTA station and the gifts he gave me. Some might not think that is much of a legacy, but it is to me. As I write this, I am making plans to hold Bunny Rabbit (#2) close to me and hear the music once again.

Memories that are treasured, last forever.

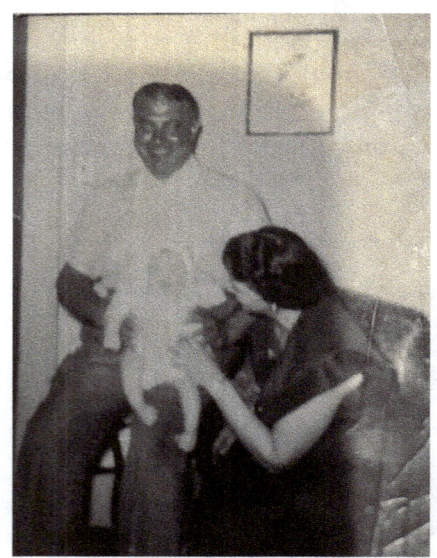

JOSEPH J. FUCILLO
OUR NEXT SENATOR

Wards 1-2-3 Boston and Ward 1 Cambridge

Chapter 6

The Relatives

Italian families are huge with numerous brothers, sisters, aunts, uncles, and cousins, really huge. Mine was not. I was an only child. That was difficult for me but I was blessed with some wonderful relatives.

Auntie Jennie

Auntie Jennie was my God Mother, and my mother was Auntie Jennie's daughter Joannie's Godmother. Auntie Jennie's real name was Giovanna. Like my mother and others at the time she anglicized her name, especially because she was called Giovannina. She became Jeanette and that turned into Jennie.

Nonna Caggiano

Tony and Nonno Caggiano

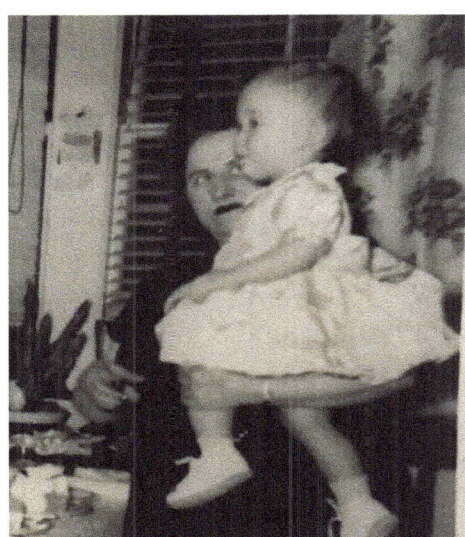

Auntie Jennie and me at my First Birthday

She was a Caggiano and the family had a flower shop on Fleet Street and then Hanover Street. Memories of Auntie Jennie's mother sitting on a crate or chair outside the shop will never leave me. She ran the store and was an iconic fixture in the North End. Her son Tony moved the shop to the beginning of Hanover Street, and it is still there under different ownership.

Auntie Jennie was a widow and lived with her two children in a three room walk up (Way Up) on Hanover Street. Mother and daughter shared the bedroom and her son shared the living room for sleeping. There are a lot of tragic stories in this small family.

Soon after having their first child, Buddy's wife died at a very young age from cancer. He had a florist shop in Medford following the family tradition. Sadly, Buddy also died before his time.

After graduating Juile Billiart High School, Auntie Jennie's daughter Joannie married into a family who had recently come from San Sossio Baronia, Avellino, and settled in East Boston. Her husband and three of his brothers, started an ice cream company. Tragically, three of the brothers, including Joannie's husband, were killed after being struck by a car while changing a tire on Route 9. I will never know how my cousin Joannie withstood the pain and in addition she was pregnant with her second child. She moved together with Auntie Jennie to a five-room apartment in West Somerville, near where my family lived. Joannie continued to work at the Ice Cream Company and Auntie Jennie took care of her two grandchildren.

When the grandchildren went to school, Auntie Jennie got a job at Cole's Drug Store in Davis Square. Every time I went there, Auntie Jennie would give me "sample" school supplies. I had the best pencil box in my class! I was maybe eight or nine years older than Maria and Joseph and when I was in college even tutored Joseph. And a couple of times I remember I was Maria's substitute teacher!

As time went on, my mother suffered from depression. I had to call Auntie Jennie to come over and help me take care of my mother. NEVER did she say she couldn't help. She had a driver's license and a car, so could get over to our house quickly. Auntie Jennie was known for her fast driving skills, and when I say quickly, I really mean really quickly. Ambulances were called, trips to hospitals, and taking care of me...she did it all. When my mother passed from cancer, Auntie Jennie's grandson, Joseph, and his cousin, helped me with cleaning out my mother's apartment. In between the times of the wake, I was at Auntie Jennie's house being fed and fed and fed some more.

The next summer I spent in Italy with Joannie's husband 's family in San Sossio Baronia, Avellino. think I got as far as Grotto Minardo by train and then had to take a taxi! I was delivered right to the door of a small two-story stucco house complete with tile roof where Zia Grazina lived. Her brother-in-law lived across the street, Zio Generoso. It was a chain of connections of families and actually I was not related to any of these people at all! But to them I became family. It is an Italian way of life! You are my brother in law's sister's nephew's widow wife's mother's godchild! *Famiglia!*

People still washed clothes in the piazza of the town at the large communal fountain. A vendor would come by the house on a donkey that had two filled baskets of tomatoes on each of its sides. The man would yell out "Pomodori" over and over again at the top of his lungs. As I love donkeys, I bought a lot of tomatoes from this man, and he was very grateful. Women would sit in front of their homes crocheting or embroidering items for a future bride. The air was fresh and sweet and the word "stress" did not seem to exist here. I learned many life lessons that summer. Most importantly: this was the way I wanted to live, simply and peacefully and I wanted to live in a town where everybody helps each other.

The next stop on my journey was Rome. In less than thirty minutes without the use of a telephone, Zia Grazina had a ride for me with a family going back to Rome the next morning. I also had the added advantage of staying in their apartment for as long as I needed. I had no clue who they were, but again I was "family" to them!

Auntie Jennie lived into her 80's and enjoyed watching her great-grandchildren and my daughter play together. She was a great cook and I use her recipe for Pizza Gaina as it must be the same as my mother's recipe, that I could never quite duplicate. Like most of my Italian female relatives, she was very opinionated. But that was what made her so much fun because I knew what was going to come out of her mouth before she said: I was doing "whatever" the wrong way! I was honored to give one of the two eulogies at her funeral.

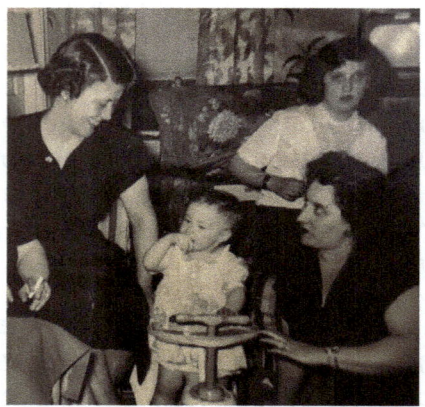

My Mother, Marie, Auntie Jennie and me

Auntie Jennie and Me - 1961

Te voglio bene sai, tanto.

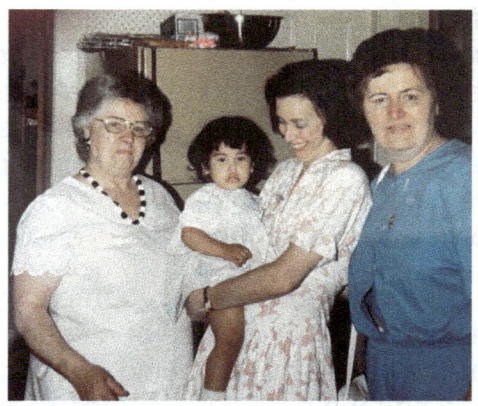

Auntie Jennie, Gabriella, Me, and Cousin Joannie - 1987

Aunt Susie, Cousin Marie her children, John and Donna

My Aunt Susie (Assunta) was three years older than my mother. She was married, had one daughter, and lived in Revere in the same house as my Great Aunt Antonetta, my grandmother's sister. Through the years my mother and my aunt's relationship was often contentious. They would have fights and hang up on each other and we would not get invited to or attend any of their family events, even my cousin's wedding.

What really hurt me was that my aunt never took care of her own mother, my Nonna. My mother always cooked, cleaned, and took care of her mother. Also, Grandma came to live with us in our new house when she could no longer live on her own.

My Mother and Aunt

Auntie Susie's house after my First Communion

I don't know the circumstances, but my aunt never visited her mother in her flat, at our house or in the Don Orione Home where Nonna spent her final days. She did not attend the wake or funeral of her mother. It became apparent that these two sisters would never reconcile. I was not the one to try and make peace, because my soul had been so scared.

One day I received a call at work from my mother. My Aunt had suddenly passed away and my mother wanted me to come home and take her to the wake. I told her that I would not go, and we had a huge fight about this. Through the emotion that was clouding any clear headedness, I gave in grudgingly. Not only did my mother go to the wake and funeral, but she also prepared all the food for the luncheon after the funeral. Why? Her answer to all of this was, "She is my sister". Just writing this makes me admire my mother so much. After all that had transpired, my mother unselfishly stepped up to do what families are supposed to do… take care of each other.

Also, some good came out of this as my cousin Marie and my mother became close. But four years later my mother would also pass. I am still close with my cousin Marie and her two married children Donna and John. I now spend the holidays with them, and we have some good laughs joking about the "old days" and of course eating delicious food just like my mother and my aunt cooked.

Cousin, Marie and husband Dominic - 1964

John and Donna

Tony and Donna - 2022

Marie, John and Donna - 2022

Donna and Gabriella - 2007

Gabriella and Uncle Dom at her High Schcol Graduation - 2005

Fucillo Family

My father had three brothers: Louis, John, and Ralph. For some reason John and Ralph moved to Rockland and were married there and raised their families. Therefore, I didn't know them very well at all. But my Uncle Louis's family moved from the North End to Chelsea and since that was close to us, we visited them a few times a year. My Uncle Louis and my Zia Michelina had five children. They all lived next to each other except Uncle Teddy who lived in Arlington. I really enjoyed visiting them as they always showed me so much love because I was Uncle Joe's daughter. All the family was very kind and loving to my mother as well and whenever I was told that we were going to visit them, my face lit up. All have passed away now. And my Aunt Eva lived to be 102 and died only a few years ago. I miss them, my only connection to my father.

My Aunt Josie Fucillo with our grandmother. Early 1920's

My Grandparents - Early 1930's

Aunt Eva and her husband, Uncle Joe Riccio at my high school graduation

Eva M. (Fucillo) Riccio

Family & friends are invited to attend Visiting Hours on Monday, April 9th from 9:00 a.m. to 11:00 a.m., in the Vertuccio & Smith, Home for Funerals, 773 Broadway (Route 107) REVERE, for Eva M. (Fucillo) Riccio, who passed in the presence of her God, serenely & peacefully, on Tuesday, April 3rd at her Chelsea residence at the privileged age of 102 years. Her Funeral Service will be conducted in the funeral home, immediately following the visitation at 11:15 a.m. and immediately followed by interment at Holy Cross Cemetery, Malden.

MRS JOSEPHINE FUCILLO DIES IN NORTH END

Mrs Josephine Fucillo, mother of Joseph Fucillo, chauffeur for Gov James M. Curley, died yesterday morning at her home, 19 Fleet st., North End, after a long sickness.

Mrs Fucillo was for years a resident of the North End, where she had lived since coming to this country from Italy more than half a century ago. She and her husband, Theodore Fusillo, who died about 3½ years ago, were among the early settlers of the Boston North End Italian colony.

Mrs Fucillo was a member of Our Lady of Lourdes Society of the Sacred Heart Church, North sq. and last evening nearly 100 women members of the society assembled at the home of the departed and recited prayers.

Mrs Fucillo is survived by four sons, Joseph, Louis, who is an assistant superintendent for a large manufacturing company; John, who was formerly chief of police at Rockland, and Ralph, who was for a number of years assistant Water Commissioner at Rockland.

The funeral will be held Friday morning at 10 o'clock, with a high mass of requiem at the Sacred Heart Church, North sq.

Cousin Stephen Da Corta

Stephen is probably my closest cousin, and only through marriage! My mother loved his family as his father was from Italy (so they could speak Italian to each other) and his mother was so welcoming every time we visited. Mama didn't like visiting people that much, so this was a big deal and said a lot about Stephen's great family.

One Easter, his whole family visited us and gave me a gift of a baby chick (back before we knew that was not a humane thing to do). During the visit Baby Chick died. We were all heartbroken and buried Baby Chick in the back yard. Stephen has a slightly different version of the "Easter Tragedy", but yes, the poor animal did die in his story too.

He has two younger sisters; one is my age and one a couple of years older. But as time went by and we were older and my parents and Stephen's father passed, we drifted apart. But Stephen and I always somehow remained close. Maybe because we both worked and lived in Boston, and we would just bump into each other randomly from time to time and rekindle our friendship. We both love cats and honor our heritage. We meet in the North End frequently and after church we enjoy a steaming hot cappuccino and a Sfogliatella that he loves but can neither spell nor pronounce.

Stephen and my dog Bosco

One Sunday after leaving the cafe, he went to his car, and I went to mine. But I couldn't find my car! I called Stephen and he was halfway home but turned around to come and rescue me! In the meantime, I asked a nearby policeman to help me.

He used the alarm on my keys, but nothing happened. So, he called in to report the car as stolen. Now, I'm panicking as I walk up and down the block on Hanover Street still looking for my car. The policeman catches up with me as Stephen arrives and of course the car is where I left it. I just missed it walking by all the black cars parked in a row. Apparently, the fob alarm wasn't working. Then Stephen, a retired Boston Police Sergeant, speaks cop talk to the policeman and all ends well. But I felt like an idiot and now take a picture of where I park!

There are few people who I can just be myself with and who also know most of my story. For me that is a very special gift. I am so grateful to have him in my life, even if he grew up in Southie and not the North End.

Stephen with wife, Linda

Stephen's mother, Aunt Lue and her sister, Aunt Sister Jeromette at my high school graduation

Dinner at Lucia's, North End with my cousins, Grandpa Uncle Tony, Uncle Mario and my daughter, Gabriella - 2004

Gabriella and Grandpa Uncle Tony celebrating her Birthday- June 2007

Chapter 7

Auntie Anna. Uncle Tony and Cousins Ron and Tony

My Mother's first cousin, Auntie Anna grew up in North Square. After she was married, the family lived on Hanover Street, almost the top floor. It was a hike to climb those stairs. Auntie Anna and her mother (my grandmother's sister, Aunt Mary) went to Italy to be with my family when my grandfather died of Tuberculosis. All I can remember is Auntie Anna saying they were there for a long time. When they arrived back from Italy, my mother and Auntie Anna attended Saint Anthony's school, but Auntie Anna didn't like the nuns at all! In fact, we learned never to mention school at the dinner table. She left school without graduating 8th grade. Mama and Auntie Anna were very close and enjoyed their time together before they were married. They loved ice skating, enjoyed going to dances and the movies. Fortunately, Auntie Anna married the kindest man to ever live on this earth, my Uncle Tony. She had the best husband in the whole family. They were blessed with two sons, my cousins Ron and Tony. Auntie Anna was small in stature but a strong-minded woman. In her younger days she was the life of the party, always ready to have some fun. Even when she was older and we were at the house for the holidays, she would say something and we would all be laughing so hard, rolling our eyes almost to the point of tears. I remember just laughing even if I had no idea what she was saying, why she said it or why she was laughing.

And "WOW" did she enjoy cooking everything imaginable for everyone! Because my cousin Ron was a TV personality, he was able to ask Dave Maynard from Chanel 4 to do a segment at the house on how to make Braciole. It was absolutely hysterical. As I recall there was a lot of wine sipping involved! "Salute!" would be said and another sip of wine followed! All this made for a great entertaining cooking lesson on preparing "Braciole", especially when she kicked Dave Maynard out of the kitchen.

My cousin Ron had this to add: "he went into the kitchen while she was cooking (a no no) and started to stir her sauce with the braciole in it. She, in her own way, strongly suggested that he leave the kitchen."

Ron had a bit more to relate: Here's the broccoli story and some others. Broccoli was cooked to the point where it was so soft it would slide through the tines of a fork. Eggplant for parmesan had to be peeled, sliced, placed in a colander with a plate over it and an iron put on top of the plate so slices of eggplant could be drained overnight before it was fried then layered for the parmesan preparation and put in the oven. Made me wonder when I was a kid what an iron from the ironing board had to do with eggplant parm. Then there were various comments to that dish and other meals she made like asking "do you want some more?" If you said no, she would say "you didn't like it?". If you said "no I did like it" you automatically got another portion on your plate. Another thing she would say if you refused more food was "have more, I'm only going to throw it away if you don't". To which my brother would say "so you're offering me swill"?

Auntie Anna, like many Italian woman during that time, worked in the garment district with friends along with my Aunt Josie. I had a lot of Aunt Josies! This Auntie Josie's son John was the first of my family to go to college! A very big accomplishment and he outdid that accomplishment by going to Dartmouth! He was the oldest child of my generation and I was the youngest, twenty years younger. I was the fourth to go to college and the first woman to do so.

As Auntie Anna aged, she became reclusive. Although my uncle would take her on Sunday drives to New Hampshire, her hesitation of leaving the house increased. The house doors were aways shut and securely locked and the venetian blinds were always closed. The house was filled with darkness. Tragically, this was a result of her childhood experiences. My great uncle was not a good man. Growing up Auntie Anna's house was filled with the darkness of domestic abuse. I never had exact details and her father passed away before I was born. My mother and Uncle Tony would tell me to stay away from Auntie Anna's brother, as he was just as bad as his father. In contrast, Zia Mariuccia (Mary), my aunt was very loving, but sadly died when I was young. Despite Auntie Anna's increasing fear of the outside world, she would perk up and did love company, especially when her two children Ron and Tony would visit.

Cousin Tony, Auntie Mary, Cousin Ron and Auntie Anna

After my mother died, I would go to their house for all the holidays except for Christmas Day, when I went to my God Mother Auntie Jennie's house. Christmas Eve was extra special to every Italian, the Feast of the Seven Fishes. Our dinner was more like the Feast of Every Fish in the Ocean! We had Shrimp, Scallops, Lobster, Quahogs, Linguini with Mussels, Calamari, Haddock, Fillet of Sole, Croquets, Stuffed Peppers.... we ate forever. And there were more than seven fishes for sure. Rum Cake and/or Zuppa Inglese with the freshest whipped cream, from Modern Pastry and Auntie Anna's Struffoli and Cenci, finished off the night along with coffee and cordials.

My fondest memory was one Christmas Eve when Auntie Anna just might have had a little too much Amaretto, maybe with a little help from us! With glass in hand, she burst into song: her favorite "Dicitencello Vuje".

> Dicitencello a 'sta cumpagna vosta
> ch'aggio perduto 'o suonno e 'a fantasia
> ch"a penzo sempe,
> ch'è tutt"a vita mia
> I' nce 'o vvulesse dicere,
> ma nun ce 'o ssaccio dí
>
> 'A voglio bene
> 'A voglio bene assaje!
> Dicitencello vuje
> ca nun mm"a scordo maje.
> E' na passione,
> cchiù forte 'e na catena,
> ca mme turmenta ll'anema
> e nun mme fa campá!

Neapolitan Language.

After another sip or two she would start singing again in a higher pitch! My next year's Christmas gift to everyone was the copy of the video I took of Auntie Anna's singing, that happiest of Christmas Eves.

When my daughter was a toddler, she would always tell Auntie Anna: "You too funny" And she was!

Auntie Anna and Gabriella - 1992

Uncle Tony was my father's best friend. I don't know how they became friends or how he met Auntie Anna. But I suspect that Uncle Tony fell in love and as they were courting, my father met my mother. Uncle Tony's family, the Polcaris, were from Montefalcione. It seemed every Polcari was from this town. Many settled on or near Sheafe Street. Uncle Tony was a storyteller. He was the keeper of the stories of our family and of life in the North End. I would learn so much from him and I wish I could have half the memory he had. One day Uncle Tony, his brothers and young friends heard an ex-plosion, a very loud explosion! They ran after the Fire Brigade rushing down Hanover Street! The young boys were almost at the end of Hanover Street but were stopped from going any further. People were running everywhere and screaming! The boys scrambled on top of a hill above Charter Street and when looking down could see what was happening. Their perch was not far from the deadly Molasses Flood of January 15, 1919. I was told the account by an actual witness to this tragedy. Now there is no witness alive to tell this story.

In May of 1908 Uncle Tony was born in the North End. He had two brothers. His brother Angelo died in World War II. Uncle Tony never got over his death. His other brother Uncle Mario married but had no children. He lived in the same apartment on Sheafe Street all his married life. His sister-in-law lived above him. Uncle Mario lived a long life and rarely strayed from the North End. But Uncle Tony was a rambling man later in life. And like Uncle Mario, Uncle Tony lived a long life, 2 months shy of 100!

Uncle Mario and Grandpa Uncle Tony. At Lucia's Restaurant on Hannover Street.

Uncle Tony attended and graduated from Saint Anthony's School. The Friars thought he had a vocation and the following year he was sent to the Junior Novitiate of the Franciscans in New York. Uncle Tony was studious, but he missed his family and did not think he wanted to become a Franciscan Friar. Consequently, after a couple of years he returned home.

He met Auntie Anna, and they married in 1930, I believe. He had been playing drums in a band, and she only agreed to marry him if he stopped playing in the band! Auntie Anna, born in 1906, was 2 years older than Uncle Tony. He also worked in the garment industry on Kneeland Street and was a cutter. He became involved in the Union and worked tirelessly to secure better working conditions for the factory workers.

Uncle Tony was outgoing. He had many friends and acquaintances. Auntie Anna was the opposite. When Uncle Tony's mother passed suddenly, his father became very distraught and needed support. Uncle Tony along with Uncle Mario, went to care for their father. Auntie Anna was very upset that he did this. She said he was giving her up and neglecting her for his father. My mother would get involved in this family drama. Mama sided with Uncle Tony but tried to get Auntie Anna to calm down. After his father passed, he went back home. The household slowly returned to normal. This was not a happy time.

One August when I was twelve, I was in the hospital having my appendix out and they both came to visit me. They brought me a light green summer bathrobe. I loved and treasured this gift and even wore it in college! They were always filled with love for my family, much like my father's family. During the holidays my cousin Ron was at their house and my cousin Tony started coming home as well. We had a great time together. I can always remember my Uncle Tony in my life. He took over the role of my father, his best friend.

Both my cousins went to Saint Anthony's School and Christopher Columbus High School. My older cousin, Tony Jr. went to Tuft University, continued to University of Chicago and married soon after. Tony's younger brother Ron went to Boston University, then Emerson College and became a professor there for a time, while starting his professional career. As a result, Auntie Anna and Uncle Tony were alone, although Uncle Tony stayed busy working in the garment industry until his mid 70's. In fact, he retired once and soon after went back to work, he said staying at home wasn't for him. They didn't socialize as a couple. But Uncle Tony had other interests. He was instrumental in starting the Arlington Senior Center as well as other organizations. He was elected as a Silver Haired Senator and received many awards for his work championing the rights of Seniors in Massachusetts. I went with him to the State Banquet where he was honored and received the award for outstanding Senior Senator. How proud he was, and I was even prouder.

When my daughter was born a new chapter started. Uncle Tony became Grandpa Uncle Tony. Cousins Tony and Ron became Gabriella's Godfathers, because how could I choose one over the other? When Uncle Tony and Auntie Anna visited us in the hospital they brought a lovely plant in a ceramic baby shoes planter, and of course food! They gushed over my daughter. Gabriella responded by sticking her tongue out at Uncle Tony. Everyone laughed and it was a story frequently told at family gatherings.

He was at every event of my daughter's life from her Christening on. He never missed a Grandparents' Day, a Dance or Piano Recital, a Birthday Party or Graduation and he said it was "his duty" to always bring the Rum Cake from Modern Pastry to every party. His love and dedication meant so much to her and to me. Every Sunday after Auntie Anna passed away, my daughter and I would either have dinner at his house and later at his condominium and then at his assisted living residence. We would end each visit by playing "Hide and Seek" until Gabriella was 'too old' to play! Many times, we went out to dinner to his favorite restaurant the Portofino in Malden. We even had his 90th birthday celebration there. Ron and Tony would be there for holidays, but my daughter and I were there every Sunday.

Me, Gabriella, Tony, Ron, and Grandpa Uncle Tony at his 90th Birthday party at Portofino's - 1998

Grandpa Uncle Tony Playing Games

Double double this this, double double that that, double double this, double that, double double this and that! We had so much fun!

Grandpa Uncle Tony needed to get more care and went to a nursing home in Cambridge. He was 99 years old! We went to Papa Razzi in Boston for Thanksgiving, 2007. Grandpa Uncle Tony was so funny and ate a lot of food! We had such a good time. He was able to come out for Christmas Eve too. We knew he was not feeling well. He passed just two months shy of his 100th Birthday in March, 2007.
I love him and miss him so much

Uncle Tony was a Traveling Man! During the winters for a couple of years he went to Florida and then he began going to Tucson for a few weeks. He went on a "Grand Tour" to Italy with my cousin Tony and among other sites visited his town of Montefalcione. He also took trips by himself including an Alaskan Cruise and Canadian Rocky Train Trip. He was frequently called by his travel agent to set up a new vacation! The biggest surprise was when he announced he was going to Saint Petersburg. I looked at him and said, "you always say you don't like Florida". He replied that he was going to Saint Petersburg in Russia! He was in his late 80's!

After having so much responsibility of a demanding marriage, two sons and work for so many years, he was having the time of his life. He was seeing the world, the town where his parents were born and the glaciers of Alaska, the Grand Canyon and the "other" Saint Petersburg!

I am so grateful you were given this time to enjoy. You were blessed to live two months shy of your 100th birthday. Gabriella had your love until she was almost 21 years old. Your bond will never be broken. I will always love you and miss your wisdom and kindness. My daughter and I were so fortunate to have you in our lives. You are the best man I ever knew. How you loved my daughter, and you will be her Grandpa Uncle Tony forever. I believe you look down on us and guide us every day.

I see trees of green, red roses too, I see them bloom for me and you. And I think to myself what a wonderful world!

CHAPTER 8

"You Don't Like the Food?"

You don't like the food? You found someplace better to eat? Go live with them.

You like the food?
    Yes I love it, but I am full.
Good here is some more. Now eat. Enjoy!

You too good for us now?

I am going to send you to the Protestant School.

I slaved all day over a hot stove.

Do you know how much that cost? EAT!

A boyfriend?, we have to meet him, he's Italian right? Do I know the family?

Be home when I say, or you will never go out again.

Are you sick? You look sick..have some soup. I just made it.
    I am not sick.
Don't argue with me, eat. Here's some fresh bread too.

Don't tell your mother.
(Grandma secretly puts her folded hand in my pocket leaving a scrunched-up dollar bill, like she was part of the Brinks robbery).

Whadya gonna do? With shoulder shrug
(Answer for anything perplexing)

I don't know them; you can't go over their house.

    Can I go over Cousin Marie's house?
Sure.. leave me all alone. It's okay.

Ma, I got accepted to college! Can I live in the dorm?
Are you trying to put me in an early grave?

I gave you everything, and this is how you treat me?
(Answer for mostly anything).

It's okay, go, have fun.... followed by curses under her breath.

I don't care if it's her birthday party, you can't go... we need to clean the house your aunt is coming tomorrow, it's a mess.
　　Ma, we cleaned yesterday.
Look at the dust, what will people say?

Here...bring this to the Nuns they all look so skinny. They must be Irish.
(I go to school with 5 packages of home-made Italian cookies and a ricotta pie. Nuns very happy!)

At Easter:
　　Ma, everyone loves the food.
Nah, they don't like it. Eva left some lasagna on her plate.
　　Ma, that was her second piece!
Well, she should eat it to make me happy.

So now you think you are a big shot, you got a fancy job, and some money. What's gonna happen to me? Where did I go wrong with you?

You wanna do things your own way, Huh? Well there's the door.

What are you crying? I'll give you something to cry about.

(When you go home, you leave with a week's worth of delicious food).

I want my containers back, here take this too (another container of eggplant) ....and don't forget the containers next week.

Finding a newspaper clipping of just about anything on the kitchen table: warning you to be careful, how to treat your family, how important respect is, how to polish the furniture, new recipe ideas, what boys really want in a girlfriend.

Dry your hair before you go out or you will get a cold !

You look like a street walker (Putana), your skirt is too short. Don't even think of leaving the house….and while you're at it take off all that makeup.

Endless horror stories of what can happen to you regardless of what you are doing; riding on the streetcar, eating other people's food (even those you knew), and getting in a car with a boy (even if you knew him) were the scariest.

Mama giving lots of hugs and kisses then maybe without a moments's notice… yelling "go to your room"!
You have no idea what went wrong.

You want to sleep at someone else's house? Are your crazy? We worked so hard to buy a nice bedroom for you! I give you everything I d dn't have.

Signs things are not going well…. all the saints' statues and pictures have been turned around and are facing the wall. This means huge trouble.

One day, you wait, just wait and your kids will do to you what you did to me.

Grandma Nonna - 1920's

My Confirmation at Saint Leonard's Church - 1961

Chapter 9

REFLECTIONS
Fitting In

When we moved out of the North End we settled in Winter Hill on the Somerville/Medford Line, an area where many Italians had also come from the North End to live. My mother wanted to send me to the Catholic Girl's School that most of their daughters attended. So off I went on a bus every morning to Winchester. I must confess that I was embarrassed by my mother's slight accent when she came to my school for meetings or events. She wore fashionable clothes and was very elegant, but when she spoke English, I cringed. I look back on that now and am so ashamed of myself for having these thoughts. Although over half my class was Italian or part Italian, no one had an accent like my mother. My parents worked so hard to send me to this school, how dare I have these thoughts? I know it was my age at the time and wanting to fit in. But I think of everything my mother lived through in her life, to have a daughter who was ashamed of her was unforgivable. My only solace is that I don't think she was ever aware of my feelings.

Values

My parents were lucky and sometimes in the right place at the right time, to have opportunities for employment and worked very hard to achieve what they had. They taught me through their actions that I too could also achieve my goals and never be limited because of my ethnicity or gender. My parents also embraced other ethnicities and races. I was raised to see all people as equals and my parents never looked down on anyone and welcomed people, all people, into our home. Frankly, I never knew who would be visiting. I will always take pride in how these values were instilled in me at an early age.

As I grew older and saw the words and actions of other adults and their families, I was sad and angry that people could act this way. Another motto I used with my students was,

"Never Forget Where You Come From". It seems that a lot of people have.

My mother and I went to Washington D.C. in the summer of 1957. My father was friends with our congressman, and we were given special passes to visit many sites in the Nation's Capital. We stayed at the Hilton Hotel and were just a short bus ride away from almost everything on our list to visit. When we were at the bus stop my mother said, "stay at the front of the bus and DO NOT SIT DOWN, even if there is an empty seat, pretend we are the next people getting off". I had no idea why she said this. I complied and every time we took a bus we stood in the front. After we came home from the trip Daddy Gene and Mama sat me down in the kitchen. I thought that I had done something wrong, as usual. Instead, it was my first lesson on racism in the United States. My father explained all about Rosa Parks, how Black people in the South had to sit in the back of the bus and give up their seat for a white person. I then realized my mother was actually trying to prevent that from happening by pretending we were the next ones getting off the bus. My mother was not a very educated person, but she had followed the news and knew what was happening in the South. She thought up this plan to allow others to sit down as she did not want anyone to give up a seat for us. To this day, every time I think of that trip to D.C., I marvel at her foresight! In her own way, she was trying to respect the rights we all should have. She was that little pebble thrown into the ocean that hopefully would ripple throughout all the oceans of the world.

Education

My parents stressed education and would tell me, it was my most valuable possession. This was the philosophy of my father who never attended school and my mother who only went to school until eighth grade. I was very fortunate to have the ability to receive a very good education and to speak two languages in my home, Neapolitan Dialect and English. Being always taught to celebrate and never be ashamed of my heritage, shaped who I am. My mother would say I was going to go to Radcliffe! At the time I had no idea what she meant, because she started telling me this when I was about six years old!

In High School, I was headed to Boston College, then my father got sick my junior year. Therefore, I had to "settle" for Salem State College. This was a blessing in disguise. I had great professors and still maintain the close friendships I made. I couldn't ask for better friends. Professor John Fox was my mentor. He encouraged me to work for my Congressman in Washington D.C., to 'dissect' the intent of the 14th Amendment and he also "lit the flame" to tape oral histories of my mother's friends in the North End! I received my graduate degree from Boston College. While there, I continued my Constitutional studies with Dr. Scigliano. He was the nephew of the North End's revered George Scigliano, who was the first person to relentlessly strive to improve the lives of Italian Immigrants at the turn of the century.

Lastly, growing up in a house with two languages helped me to also become fluent in Spanish, which furthered my career and start my own Educational Sales and Consulting Company.

Without my parents always pushing me to do my best, I do not think I would have achieved what I did. I remember my father looking at one of my report cards and telling me, "You can do better". I replied "Daddy, I got all A's". That did not deter him from saying, "You still can do better!". I am indebted to them for their guidance, encouragement, and support. There was never a discussion of "if" I went to college. The discussion was "where"' would I go to college.

Being Italian

Being Italian comes with responsibility to my immediate and extended family. I can bring no shame to my family. I must kiss and hug every family member I know, except the one my mother told me never to go near. We must be together for Sunday Dinner and bring friends.

In my family, my mother worked two days and two nights a week, so I had to learn how to cook what my mother cooked, but just the simple recipes. She was top chef! I needed to keep the house spotless. Every day when I came home from school there was a "list of chores" sitting on the kitchen table. If my mother was working late, the list would include what to cook for dinner and then do the cleanup. I listened to Perry Como, Jerry Vale, Sergio Franchi, Al Martino, Connie Francis, Dean Martin, Tony Bennett, Mario Lanza and any other singer who was Italian, as my mother played their albums on the record player while she was cooking. She cooked incessantly, but that is Being Italian. And the cooking led to a large array of food that was placed on the table, which was covered with an "extra special" tablecloth. No one could ever consume that much food. But the continuous commands to "eat" still came from my mother's mouth.

Mama was devoted to Grandma, and both were devoted to Saint Anthony. To see statues and framed pictures of Saint Anthony around the house was a part of Italian interior decorating. Thankfully, we had no plastic on the furniture. We "adapted" and put plastic on the rugs!

Throughout my childhood, if I wasn't paying attention to my mother, she would say, "Who am I, Saint Anthony preaching to the fishes?"

My favorite Saint Anthony Painting: Preaching to the Fishes

Visiting my extended family, making numerous trips to wakes, funerals and bringing flowers to the cemetery many times throughout the year, was not optional. But again, that is Being Italian.

During Christmas time we didn't put up our tree until the Sunday before Christmas Eve. When my grandmother and her family first came to Boston in 1901, the Nativity was among the possessions they brought with them. The Nativity was displayed Christmas Eve. This was a very special night, bigger than Christmas Day, because we had the Feast of the Seven

Fishes. Every fish imaginable was cooked to perfection and carefully placed on the table, covered with the Christmas Tablecloth for this special night. Thankfully, my mother would not cook eel. It wasn't until early Christmas morning that Baby Jesus was put in the Nativity.

Another tradition from Italy was the Feast of the Three Kings on January 6th. That was to celebrate the Three Kings arriving to see Baby Jesus and bring Him gifts. So the Kings and camels would be added to the Nativity. We all received a small present too and a special cake. If the slice you got had a coin in it, you received more blessings from the Baby Jesus. So that is Being Italian during Christmas time, it lasted awhile!

I continue the tradition with the same Nativity my family brought from Italy

Joy and Sorrow

There was joy and sorrow in my family. Both will not leave my memory and my heart hurts deeply. Memories that are painful have long lasting effects. But I try to balance that by remembering the happy times we shared. I loved the singing and dancing, especially the Tarantella which I could actually do and the waltz that my mother gave up trying to teach me. What fun I had playing tricks on my mother with my Nonna at my side. We would take all my mother's shoes and hide them! There were times my mother would take me on the train to Revere Beach and maybe meet a relative or two there. Or we would go downtown to Jordan Marsh and visit the toy department and then go to Boston Common and feed the pigeons. I need to think of these times when we laughed so hard, we cried. Though sometimes it is hard to find that balance.

The life of immigrants was filled with "Hardship and Hope", not the stereotype the North End is always characterized by "Food and Feasts". The majority of immigrants improved their lives by coming to America. But many did not, they were filled with despair, disappointment, and desperation. They experienced discrimination and distrust. We must remember all those that did not achieve the dream. These immigrants were so consumed with sadness that they fell into an abyss that changed their lives forever and could never find their way out. Their stories too, should never be forgotten.

Pride, Soul & Blood

I am proud of my heritage and I am proud to have been born in the North End. Even after we moved, we were there three times a week taking care of my Nonna, and I was there with her in the summers and school vacations. My memories are always with me. I can still conjure up the smells of Iacopucci's, my aunt's flower shop, the fish market and best of all the bakeries and pastry stores. I still hear the neighbors yelling to each other through open windows or the boys riding on their home-made scooters. I can see the ice man sweating and struggling up the three flights of stairs to my Nonna's flat. I can still feel the joy of running around the Prado chasing the pigeons, lighting candles at the Grotto, going to Clayman's and gazing at a colorfully printed tablecloth and going to the feast and wanting to be the angel. I still taste the sandwiches from Iacopucci's and the Friday night quahogs and all my mother's delicious food. I still see the faces of the kids I played skip ball and hopscotch with on the sidewalks. I still feel the pain walking home from Haymarket or Salem Street lugging the heavy bags of fresh vegetables, fruits, meat, or fish and how my fingers would hurt getting those nails out of my Nonna's crates. What joy it was to be outside on my fire escape knowing everyone, and everyone knowing and watching out for me. I still feel the security of knowing my extended family was always nearby, and all the love that we shared.

But what I miss most is my grandmother and going to Saint Anthony's, hand in hand with her as she dragged me across Hanover Street. Now every week I am usually in the North End and I feel her spirit and her hand grasping mine. Looking at my house on Fleet Street, I am filled with a sense of belonging, however bittersweet. If a person tells me that they are from the North End, a floodgate opens, and the unfortunate person is drowned in questions. But more likely than not, we will find a connection. To me that is so "old world" and perhaps just unique to this small, .36 square mile section of Boston called the North End. There is pride in being from that area, something that I can't explain. It is intangible, it is in my blood, inside my soul. And I know that joy, that contentment, that spiritual feeling of connection will never leave me, in fact it sustains me.

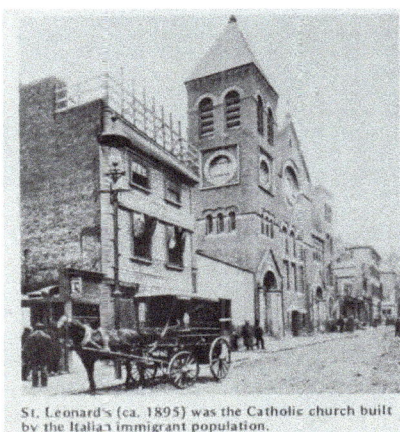

St. Leonard's (ca. 1895) was the Catholic church built by the Italian immigrant population.

Airola, Benevento

San Sossio Baronia, Avellino; Feast of Madonna Delle Grazie (Saint Leonard's Church)

Chapter 10

Research and Documents

I began my family research with the documents and photographs my mother had saved about her family and my father's family. I then went on Ancestry and compiled a family tree and obtained ship manifests, census records and church records that would help piece together my family's journeys.

But since my family was relatively new to America, I really needed to get Italian documents. This need led me to town offices in Italy. Some of the phone calls were hysterical. But all of these calls were dead ends other than someone in the town office saying, "Oh, I knew your family"! Considering the number of Fuccillos in Chiusano that wasn't very helpful. The Fuccillos n the North End (all from Chiusano) are still trying to figure out how we are all related! We are all family because this town is not large at all. A friend of mine, Norma is a Fuccillo and a Reppucci from Chiusano, as am I on my father's side, and we don't know how we are related. I am determined to piece everything together. It takes a lot of research, especially when the surnames are spelled differently, because of illiteracy or carelessness on the part of clerks or officials compiling various forms and documents.

So, I migrated to a very informative site in Italy called Antenati. I can go into this town of 2000 people and find records (death, birth, marriage etc.) going back centuries. Remembering this is Italy, I was not expecting to see such precise information! I went to the 1700's and stopped. All the important records I need are handwritten and difficult to decipher. All records are in volumes by year, some beginning and ending months could be in the preceding or following volumes. Some volumes have an index, which is a great help. But again, I found the index could be compiled by using first names or last names. Although helpful, it is very time consuming. It was very difficult to find my grandfather's siblings, However, I could find his father! I will go back to the archives and trace down the Fuccillo's extensive roots. That is my next project.

Fuccillo, Fucillo, Iucillo, Tucillo!

Family Tree: Fucillo/Reppucci

My grandparents went back to Italy due to a death in family This is the Vancouver Manifest of their return in 1903.

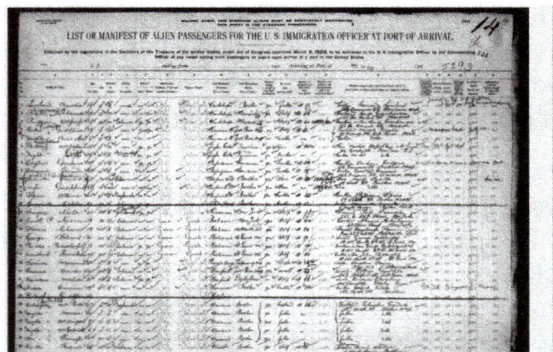

Everyone lives at 19 Fleet Street, North End

Birth Record of my Great Grandmother Maddalena Cataldo, Indicating her father, Pasquale Cataldo. My Great Great Grandfather

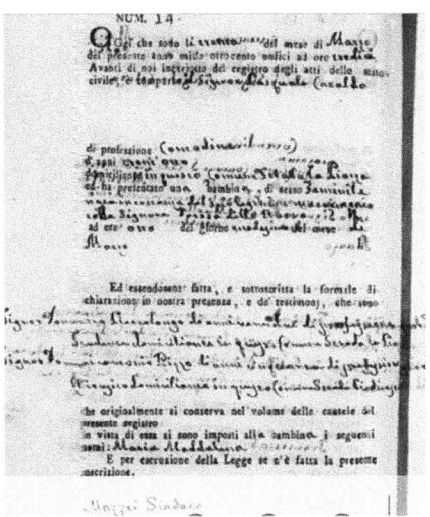

Birth Record of my Great Grandfather Leonardo Reppucci Indicating his father, Giovanni Reppucci. My Great Great Grandfather.

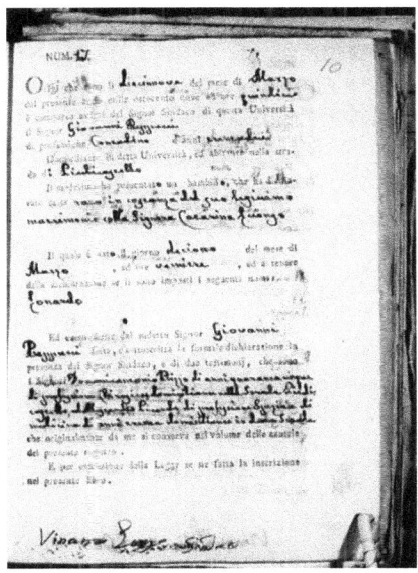

Birth Record of my Grandfather Teodoro Fuccillo. Indicating his father, Luigi Fuccillo. My Great Grandfather

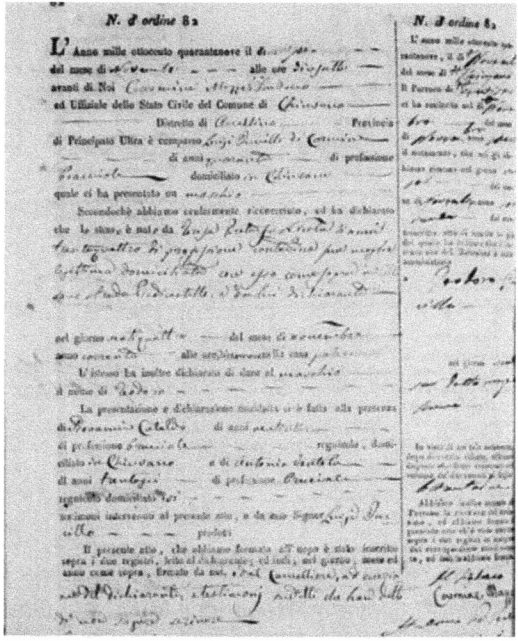

Ship Manifest, June 3, 1891

My Grandmother Giusippina and my three Uncles, Luigi, Raffaele and Giovanni. # 894, #895, #896 #897arrive from Chiusano de San Domenico via Naples to Ellis Island. Ship: Alsatia

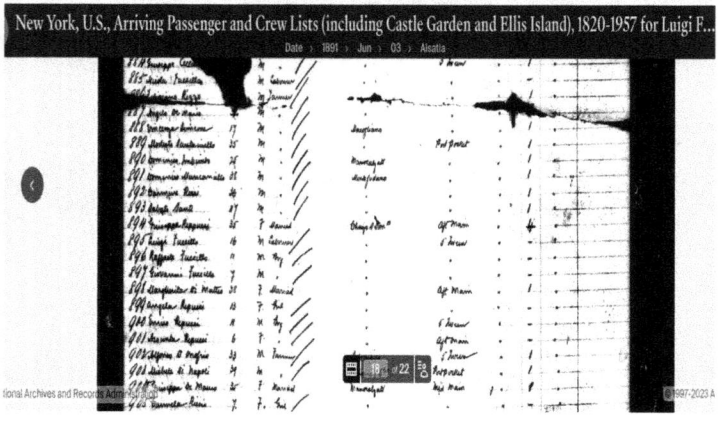

Toto/ Iuliucci Family Tree

My Grandmother's Birth Certificate

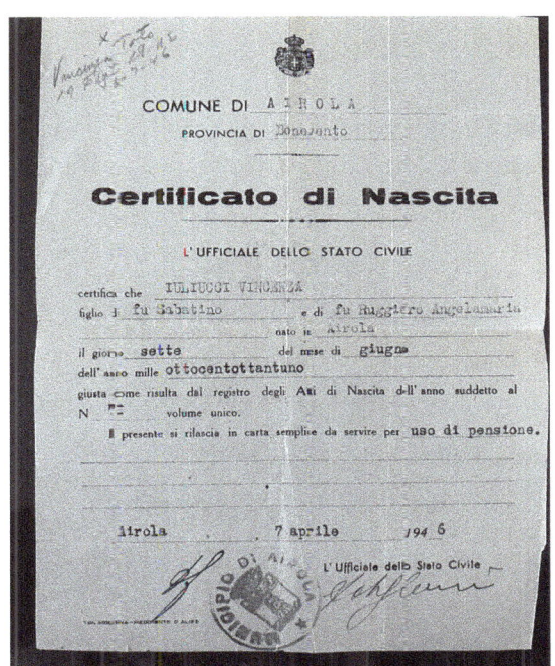

Ship Manifest Hesperia: Manifest

My Great Grandparents and their three daughters.

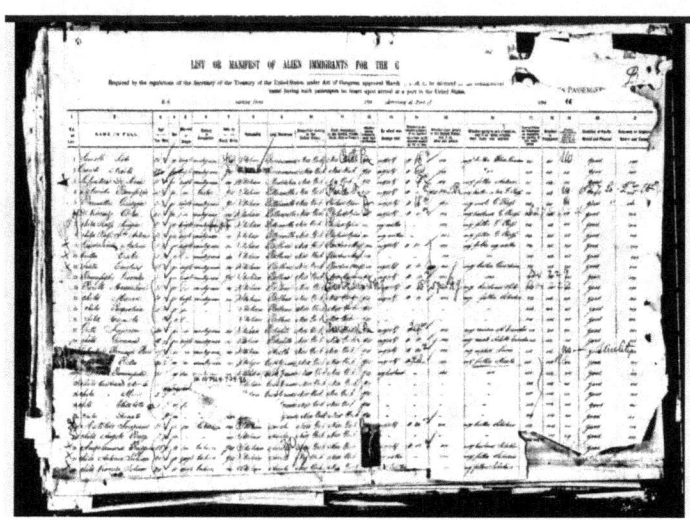

My Great Grandfather: Although he had a fairly good job in Benevento, he came to Boston and shined shoes.

Name:	Sabatino Iuliucci
Residence Year:	1916
Street Address:	364 North
Residence Place:	Boston, Massachusetts, USA
Occupation:	Bootblack
Publication Title:	Boston, Massachusetts, City Directory, 1916

My Grandfather, Michele Toto

Marriage Certificate
Saint Leonard s Church 1909

Nonna became a Third Order of Saint Francis

TERZ'ORDINE DI SAN FRANCESCO D'ASSISI
Provincia dell' Immacolata Concezione
New York, N.Y.

Fratello / Sorella: Vincenza Tota
Indirizzo: 19 Fleet St. Boston, Mass.
Data di Recezione: May 5, 1918
Data di Professione: June 8, 1919
Chiesa: St. Leonard's
Città: Boston   Stato: Mass.
Direttore: Fr Benjamin O.F.M.
Data: August 24, 1953

Italian "Enemy Aliens" had to take a Loyalty Oath

Form N-438

U. S. DEPARTMENT OF JUSTICE
IMMIGRATION AND NATURALIZATION SERVICE

Court Number: 1500
Petition Number: 272608

CERTIFICATE OF LOYALTY

WHEREAS the President of the United States, acting under and by virtue of the authority vested in him by Paragraph (d), Section 326 of the Nationality Act of 1940 (54 Stat. 1150; 8 U.S.C. 726) has by Executive Order No. 9372 dated August 27, 1943, excepted from the classification of "alien enemy" all persons whom the appropriate District Director of Immigration and Naturalization shall, after investigation fully establishing their loyalty, certify as persons loyal to the United States; and

WHEREAS investigation fully establishes that the applicant named below is a person loyal to the United States;

NOW, THEREFORE, I, the undersigned, acting pursuant to and by virtue of the discretion vested in me by the President of the United States in the Executive Order hereinbefore referred to, do hereby certify VINCENZA TOTO to be a person loyal to the United States and as such entitled to exception from the classification of "alien enemy" for the sole and only purpose of applying for naturalization as a citizen of the United States.

IN WITNESS WHEREOF, I have hereunto set my hand at BOSTON, MASS, this EIGHTH day of APRIL in the year of our Lord one thousand nine hundred forty FOUR.

District Director of Immigration and Naturalization.

Grandma's Declaration of Intention

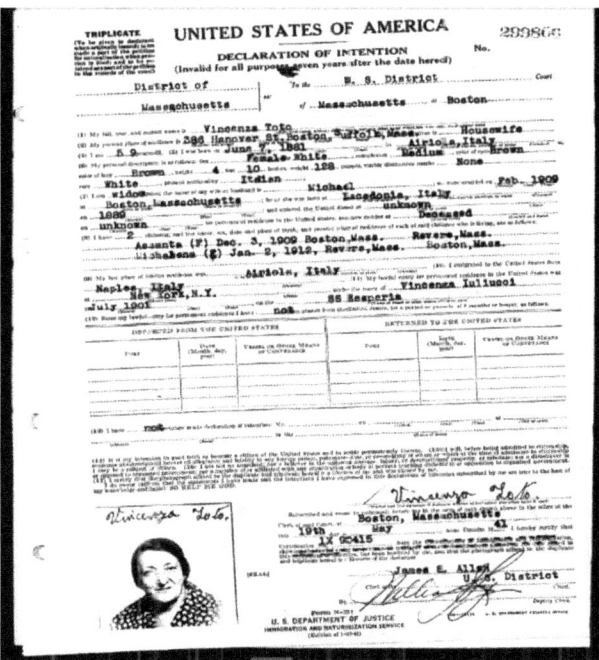

Nonna becomes a United States Citizen

Epilogue

Remembering my life in the North End, writing my stories and looking at so many photographs has brought me back to another time in my life I rarely visit. Some stories I wish never happened, while other stories bring me joy, long forgotten as if I were another person in another universe. There are emotions that explode in my head and I wish I could erase them from my memory. I must accept the sorrow and counter it with joy. However, the memories that bring a smile to my face should never be lost. I must play the record, sing that song, feed the pigeons and dance the Tarantella. There was joy along with the sorrow and the joy will win the battle of emotions because I will keep it alive.

I don't want the stories of my immigrant family to be forgotten. It would be disrespectful to them. My family gave up everything to come to America, and they struggled, each family having its own burdens to bear. That time in history that I was privileged to be a small part of needs to be preserved. Why should it be buried when I, in a small way, can help to keep it alive? Their stories must be told. If not, that incredible era in history, the Age of Immigration filled with blood, sweat and tears, will fade away and die.

Without my family this small glimpse into the "Old" North End could never have happened! Thank you and I love you all.

'A voglio bene
'A voglio bene assaje!
Dicitencello vuje
ca nun mm"a scordo maje
Si' tu chesta catena
ca nun se spezza maje

Neapolitan Language

About The Author

Margaret (Peggy) Fucillo was born in Boston's North End. Her mother's family was from Airola, Benevento and Lacedonia, Avellino. All her father's family was from Chiusano di San Domenico, Avellino. Although her family would later move from the North End to the neighboring city, she was constantly in the North End. Along with her mother, she cared for her grandmother visited relatives and attended church.

She was the first woman of her generation to attend college She continued to earn M.A. in Political Science from Boston College and did graduate work at Harvard University. Fluent in Spanish, she spent many years in urban school districts teaching newly arrived immigrants English as a Second Language as well as Spanish. Her consulting company provided Professional Development in Second Language Acquisition and Multicultural Education to school districts throughout New England and Puerto Rico. She has presented at both National and Regional Bilingual Education and English as a Second Language Conferences. Recently, she was Adjunct Faculty at North Shore Community College.

She is a member of the North End Historical Society and a Parishioner at Saint Leonard's Church in the North End.

Chiusano di San Domenico, Avellino

For Further Reading and Information

Una Storia Segreta: The Secret History of Italian American Evacuation and Internment during World War II Paperback – Illustrated, May 1, 2001. by <u>Lawrence DiStasi</u> (Author), <u>Sandra M. Gilbert</u> (Foreword)

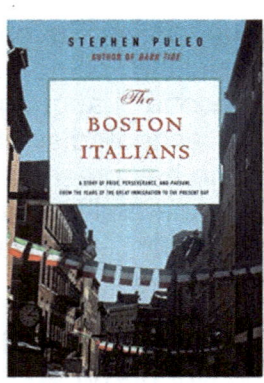

The Boston Italians: A Story of Pride, Perseverance, and Paesani, from the Years of the Great Immigration to the Present Day by Stephen Puelo | May 1, 2008

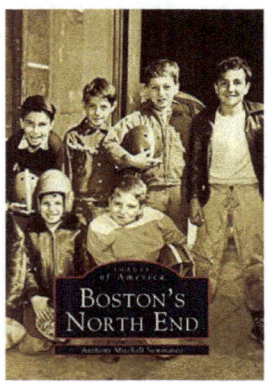

Boston's North End (MA) (Images of America) by Anthony Mitchell Sammarco | Apr 28, 2004

Boston's North End: Images and Recollections of an Italian-American Neighborhood Paperback – January 1, 2006 by Anthony V. Riccio (Author)

From Italy to the North End
Photographs, 1972-1982
By Anthony V. Riccio
Foreword by James S. Pasto

Stories, Streets, and Saints: Photographs and Oral Histories from Boston's North End. 2022 by Anthony V. Riccio (Author), Nicholas Dello Russo, (Foreword) James Pasto (Contributor)'

https://www.northendboston.org/copy-of-blog